Foreword

During the 1990s, surveys of drug misuse on the part of the general population have come of age. The drugs self-report component of the British Crime Survey has played an important part in that development.

Surprising as it may seem, this is the first time, in this country, that two consistently gathered sets of self-report drugs data from large-scale surveys of the public have been assembled for publication. The results show that drug misuse has not been increasing across the whole of England and Wales, between the 1994 and 1996 British Crime Survey. There is however some regional variation.

CHRISTOPHER NUTTALL
Director of Research and Statistics

July 1997

Acknowledgements

This report has been even more of a team effort than the previous one concerned with drug misuse, from the perspective of the British Crime Survey. All of the the regular group working with the British Crime Survey has helped with this report. Particular thanks go to Andrew Percy, while Pat Mayhew, Catriona Mirrlees-Black and Sarah Partridge have made useful contributions. Margaret Allday helped to get the Appendices into shape.

As usual, colleagues in other parts of the Home Office, especially in Action Against Drugs Unit and the Central Drugs Prevention Unit, have provided helpful feedback, as have staff of the Central Drugs Coordination Unit.

MALCOLM RAMSAY
JOSEPHINE SPILLER

Drug Misuse Declared in 1996: latest results from the British Crime Survey

by

Malcolm Ramsay and Josephine Spiller

A Research and Statistics Directorate Report

Home Office
Research and
Statistics
Directorate

London: Home Office

Home Office Research Studies

The Home Office Research Studies are reports on research undertaken by or on behalf of the Home Office. They cover the range of subjects for which the Home Secretary has responsibility. Titles in the series are listed at the back of this report (copies are available from the address on the back cover). Other publications produced by the Research and Statistics Directorate include Research Findings, Statistical Bulletins and Statistical Papers.

The Research and Statistics Directorate

The Directorate consists of three Units which deal with research and statistics on Crime and Criminal Justice, Offenders and Corrections, Immigration and General Matters; the Programme Development Unit; the Economics Unit; and the Operational Research Unit.

 The Research and Statistics Directorate is an integral part of the Home Office, serving the Ministers and the department itself, its services, Parliament and the public through research, development and statistics. Information and knowledge from these sources informs policy development and the management of programmes; their dissemination improves wider public understanding of matters of Home Office concern.

First published 1997

Application for reproduction should be made to the Information and Publications Group, Room 201, Home Office, 50 Queen Anne's Gate, London SW1H 9AT

Contents

Summary

Surveys of the general public have emerged during the 1990s as an important new source of information on drug misuse. Complemented by school surveys, they have highlighted the extent of drug taking, and leave us much better informed than before about pattens of drug misuse, whether by young people or by older generations.

The British Crime Survey (BCS) is a large survey representative of the general public in England and Wales, which focuses mainly but not entirely on victimisation. It first carried a wide-ranging drugs self-report component in 1992. This initial exercise took a traditional form, with a paper questionnaire for self-completion. For the 1994 and 1996 sweeps of the BCS, interviewees completed the drugs self-report component on laptop computers handed over to them by their interviewers. This physical switch may have helped to demarcate the drugs component from the other parts of the survey. The results from this self-keying certainly seem more reliable than those from the 1992 BCS. And because precisely the same self-report method was used in the 1994 and 1996 BCS, together with identical sampling techniques, it is possible, for the first time, to make valid comparisons between surveys carried out in different years.

Anyone specifically interested in that comparison will need to turn to Chapter 3, or to the relevant part of this summary, which covers each of the five chapters in turn.

Introduction: the nuts and bolts of this survey (Chapter 1)

The 1996 BCS had a core sample of some 16,500 people aged 16 and over, representative of the population of England and Wales. The response rate was high for a national survey, at 83 per cent. Like other surveys of its kind, it excludes the homeless and those living in institutional settings, whose drug misuse may differ from that of the general population.

The drugs self-report component of the BCS was only completed by those aged 16–59. While three per cent of eligible interviewees opted out, there were 10,940 active participants.

As well as the core sample, there was an ethnic 'booster' sample to increase the total number of minority respondents. This makes it possible to assess how drug consumption varies across different ethnic groups. However, the booster sample is not deployed in Chapters 2 and 3, in which the main findings of this report are presented.

Findings from the 1996 BCS (Chapter 2)

The main findings were:

- On any fairly recent basis, drug misuse is comparatively rare. Although nearly one in two of those aged 16–29 have at some point tried a prohibited drug, last-year and last-month consumption is much less common, at around one in four (last year) and one in seven (last month) respectively.

- For many, drug misuse simply involves cannabis. Over half of all young people reporting drug misuse within the last month have only taken cannabis.

- No other drug is as widely consumed as cannabis. Within the 16–29 age group, it has been taken at some point by 36 per cent; in the last year by 21 per cent and in the last month by 12 per cent.

- By contrast, one or more of a range of 'hallucinants' (amphetamine, LSD, magic mushrooms, ecstasy and poppers), sometimes associated with party-going and clubbing by young people, has been tried by just over a quarter (26%) at some point in their lives; by 11 per cent in the last year, and by five per cent in the last month. For the very youngest, those still in their late teens, the equivalent figure, for consumption of any of those drugs within the last year, was a higher one, at 16 per cent. Interestingly, while the media has concentrated on ecstasy, it is the least popular of these drugs for the full 16–29 age range (and second least popular for the 16–19 group, for whom magic mushrooms are least popular).

- Consumption by individuals of a range of different drugs – that is, more than just one or two substances within any of the three recall periods – is also comparatively rare. Among 16–29 year olds, 17 per cent have taken three or more different drugs on a lifetime basis; equivalent figures for the last year and month were six per cent and two per cent respectively.

- Consumption of heroin or of crack cocaine, on a lifetime footing or otherwise, was extremely rare, even bearing in mind some possible under-reporting. Only one per cent of 16–29s declared that they had ever taken heroin; a similar proportion admitted to taking crack at some point in their lives. However, if one focuses on a wider group of potentially allied substances – heroin, cocaine, crack and methadone (the latter being a synthetic opiate) – five per cent of this same age group have ever tried one or another.

The remainder of the chapter shifts in focus to characteristics of people more likely to be involved in drug misuse. In general, drug misuse is spread quite widely among all manner of people: there are no risk-free groups, at least within the younger age range. However, there are a number of important differentiating factors, including:

- age (both across the sample and within the 16–29 group, with those aged 20–24 having a particularly high rate, at 49 per cent for any drug, ever)

- gender (more drug misuse by males)

- drinking and smoking behaviour (more drug misuse by drinkers and smokers)

- socio-economic variables such as income and employment status (important but complex links between these variables and drug misuse)

- lifestyle options, such as frequency of going out in evenings (young people with more outgoing lifestyles were at greater risk of drug misuse).

These factors are all significantly associated with patterns of drug misuse.

The 1994 and 1996 BCS compared (Chapter 3)

For the first time, change in drug prevalence can now be measured reliably by the BCS. Consumption of drugs on a last-year footing provides the best yardstick.

The two sets of 'last-year' findings show an absence of significant change, across England and Wales as a whole. This is true of the 16–29 age group as well as the full age range. Even looking at consumption of individual drugs, as opposed to any drug, all changes, upwards and downwards, were non-significant (no more than 1%).

At regional level, the picture was more complicated. There was a significant reduction in last year consumption of any drug in London by the 16–19 age group. This was offset by a significant increase across the Midlands/North, on the part of the broader 16–29 age group.

ACORN housing categories and ethnicity (Chapter 4)

ACORN (A Classification of Residential Areas) combines housing characteristics for different areas with their economic status.

ACORN has six basic categories, one of which – Rising – has significantly higher rates of drug misuse than the other five, irrespective of age group. Rising areas are urban ones populated by professional people, who tend to have active and varied leisure lives. Those living in Rising areas are more at risk of drug misuse even than those in impoverished areas with a high proportion of council housing (Striving). The sole – limited – exception to this generalisation is that a particular subcategory within the Striving classification, covering areas of high unemployment, has rates of drug misuse in line with those for the Rising category as a whole, but less than those of one particular subcategory within the Rising classification which has the highest level of all (better-off executive areas, in inner-city settings).

Findings on ethnicity echo those of the previous BCS. Whites have the highest levels of misuse; Afro-Caribbeans the next highest; while Indians and Pakistanis/Bangladeshis have the lowest levels. Only with heroin and crack is there any closing of the gaps: across the full 16–59 age range, one per cent of whites, Afro-Caribbeans and Pakistanis/Bangladeshis all reported consumption of heroin at some point in their lives, as was also the case with crack.

Assessment of changing drug misuse by different ethnic groups, between the 1994 and 1996 BCS, is not entirely straightforward. But the general picture for both 16–29s and the full 16–59 age group is one of stability, with no significant changes on the part of any ethnic group.

Discussion/implications (Chapter 5)

Household surveys need to be handled with care. It is easy to over-emphasise the fact that roughly one in two young people have tried a prohibited drug at some point in their lives. This does not mean that drug misuse should count as normal behaviour. In the first place, the proportion taking drugs with any regularity – that is, on a last-month footing – is much less, at around one in seven. Secondly, other self-report research has shown that just as many young people have committed other types of criminal offences as have taken drugs (Graham and Bowling, 1995); young people have always been apt to engage in occasional deviant acts. Thirdly, the climate of opinion among young people in relation to drugs is not necessarily permissive (Shiner and Newburn, 1996); a majority is still opposed to legalisation (Ramsay, 1994b).

Finally, the BCS is helping to chart the impact of the newly-enhanced drugs strategy. Under the 1995 White Paper, *Tackling Drugs Together,* levels of drug misuse by under 25s constitute a Key Performance Indicator (H.M. Government, 1995). Across England and Wales as a whole, consumption of any prohibited drug within the last year, on the part of the 16–24 age group, stayed the same between the 1994 and 1996 BCS. This points to favourable circumstances for the drugs strategy, across society at large. The next sweep of the BCS, to be carried out in 1998, will update that assessment.

1 Introduction

A user's guide to the report

Is drug misuse increasing? Is it worsening, with greater consumption of particularly harmful drugs? These are important questions for policy-makers (H.M. Government, 1995); they are also of widespread concern to the general public (Grace, 1996).

It is easy to be pessimistic. The smoking, swallowing, sniffing and sometimes injecting or other ingestion of prohibited drugs is certainly more widespread than it was, say, 40 years ago. Even the range of forbidden substances has widened. However, it is not straightforward to measure change in drug misuse. Annual or six monthly statistics on "registered addicts" or on "people presenting to services for problem drug misuse" have been collected for some time. Yet such figures are best seen for what they are – as a census of misusers undergoing treatment – rather than as a guide to the true extent of drug misuse. One important complicating factor is that only a very small proportion of even regular drug misusers seek treatment. The rest go unrecorded.

Another way of measuring the extent of drug misuse, pursued here, is through surveys of the general population. Of course, surveys are also likely to underestimate the prevalence of drug misuse. Their coverage of the homeless, or those living in institutions, is likely to be limited. And the more chaotic drug misusers are not easily contactable by survey interviewers.

Nonetheless, surveys have important advantages. The range of social variables that can be accessed is generally much greater than with succinct medical details compiled by busy treatment staff. In so far as drug misusers can be said to be particular kinds of people, their social characteristics have a surprising amount in common, irrespective even of their frequency of misuse (Ramsay and Percy, 1996).

Survey methods continue to improve. The use of laptop computers by respondents, to input their own answers to drugs self-report questions, is an important – relatively new – development. Much of the rest of this first chapter outlines the survey methods used in the 1996 British Crime Survey.

The second chapter of this report gives an up-to-date snapshot of patterns of drug misuse in England and Wales. The standpoint is that of the 1996 British Crime Survey, which provides the very latest findings.

Surveys are also extremely well suited to measuring change over time, providing the same format continues to be followed. Particularly in the United States, where drug misuse has been problematic over a longer period of time than in this country, regular surveys of the general population have been carried out to gauge the prevalence of drug misuse. Indeed, the US National Household Survey on Drug Abuse has become extremely well established in that role, as *the* yardstick for measuring the success or failure of the government's drugs policy in that country (Harrison, 1995). While surveys have their limitations, these are not likely to change rapidly. By contrast, the availability of better treatment facilities, offering substitute prescribing and other benefits, may well draw proportionately more misusers into treatment quite rapidly, thereby influencing the relevant statistical series.

The third chapter of this report examines changes in the level of drug misuse evident over the two–year period between the last two sweeps of the British Crime Survey, as carried out in 1996 and 1994 respectively. While there were drugs self-report components in the British Crime Survey before then, these were not fully comparable. It has taken time and effort to establish a satisfactory format. Only now, for the first time, can a two-year trend be presented.

The fourth chapter has two additional perspectives, each relatively self-contained. The first of these is the ACORN classification of different areas (which, roughly speaking, combines housing characteristics with economic indicators); the second, ethnicity. With each, there is an assessment both of current patterns and of any change as measured by the 1994 and 1996 surveys.

Finally, the fifth chapter discusses the measurement of drugs misuse by means of household surveys and other approaches. The 1994 and 1996 sweeps of the British Crime Survey have an important role in tracking the progress of drugs policy (H.M. Government, 1995).

Measuring drug misuse: self-keying of laptop computers

The British Crime Survey (BCS, from now on) is designed mainly to measure people's experience of falling victim to crime against themselves or their households. It also includes other topics of interest to the Home Office, such as fear of crime. An effective self-report format for the drugs component has evolved gradually. In 1982 (the first BCS) and 1984, questions about taking cannabis were included in a self-report component otherwise given over to a number of non-drug offences. The full range of prohibited drugs was first covered in the 1992 BCS, by means of a 'tick-box' self-report booklet devoted exclusively to drugs. This was considerably more useful, although the resulting estimates were still judged "on the low side" (Mott and Mirrlees-Black, 1995).

For the next BCS, in 1994, a more sophisticated technique was employed, very much at the cutting edge of survey methodology. This involved self-keying of answers, by interviewees, on a laptop computer handed over to them by the interviewer. Instead of completing a paper questionnaire, participants work their way through a sequence of on-screen questions, responding with a 'yes', 'no' or 'don't know'; or alternatively selecting a 'don't want to answer' option. First they are asked whether they have heard of each type of drug. Then, for those drugs that they have heard of, they are also asked whether they have ever used them. Next, for drugs they have ever used, they are asked whether they have used them in the last year. For drugs used in the last year there are, additionally, questions as to use in the last month.

Here is the list, with the street names displayed on-screen:

- Amphetamines (speed, whiz, uppers)
- Cannabis (marijuana, grass, hash, ganja, blow, draw, skunk)
- Cocaine (coke)
- Crack (rock, stone)
- Ecstasy (E)
- Heroin (smack, skag, H)
- LSD (acid)
- Magic mushrooms
- Methadone or physeptone, not prescribed by a doctor
- Semeron
- Tranquillisers such as Temazepam or Valium, not prescribed by a doctor
- Amyl nitrite or poppers
- Anabolic steroids or steroids

- Glues, solvents, gas or aerosols, to sniff or inhale
- Pills or powders, which you don't know what they were
- Smoked something, excluding tobacco, which you didn't know what it was
- Anything else which you thought was a drug, not prescribed by a doctor.

A final question was added for the 1996 BCS, on injecting as a method of consumption: results are discussed in the next chapter, and in Appendix D. Readers may be puzzled by the inclusion of a drug of which they have probably never heard: Semeron. This is a bogus substance, included to check for accidental or deliberate over-claiming. The last four items listed above were excluded from the initial set of questions on knowledge of drugs ('heard of...').

The validity of self-keying was discussed in detail in the report on the 1994 BCS (Ramsay and Percy, 1996). This time round, only some key points are outlined below, with further analysis confined to Appendix A.

• Over-claiming was extremely rare in the 1996 BCS (as in the 1994 BCS). This is where Semeron, the bogus drug, is a useful indicator. Out of a total sample of over 10,000, only five people in the 1996 BCS claimed ever to have tried it.

• Under-reporting was rare. One sign is that "don't want to answer" responses to questions about ever using particular drugs were very rare, runnning at one per cent or less of the especially important 16–29 age group, for all types of drugs except cannabis and amphetamine, for which two per cent were reluctant to disclose any information.

• Interviewers only had to help out a very small proportion of interviewees: just five per cent. In other words, 95 per cent of those who tackled the drugs self-report component using laptop computers were able to do so unaided.

The validity of the patterns of answers can be compared both with those from other surveys and, this time, by looking back at the 1994 BCS. The general level of consistency between the two matching self-report components of the BCS, both with self-keying, was extremely high, not just in terms of the amount of drug misuse reported but also in the way this varied against vital demographic and lifestyle variables as discussed in the next chapter. This can be confirmed by referring to the report on the 1994 BCS (Ramsay and Percy, 1996). That report also contains a discussion of other surveys, as does a separate article (Ramsay and Percy, 1997). One particular survey that does need mentioning here is the National Drugs Campaign Survey (NDCS). Carried out in both 1995 and 1996, this is a survey of young people in England, in the 11 to 35 age range (although in 1995 interviewing was not organised on a random/representative basis). Results from the 1995 NDCS have been published and are broadly in line with those from the BCS (HEA/BMRB, 1996; HEA/BMRB, 1997).

Other things you may need to know about the 1996 BCS

The BCS is a nationally representative household survey of the population of England and Wales. In 1996 the core sample comprised almost 16,500 people, aged 16 and over. The number is a substantial one, even for a 'national' survey, providing reasonable coverage of a wide range of demograhic variables, down at least to regional level. Below that level, numbers tend to be too small for statistical purposes.

There are two key points about the number of people participating in the drugs component of the 1996 BCS:

• For the drugs element, only those aged 16–59 were asked to take part. This restriction also applied to the drugs component of the 1994 BCS (and of the 1992 BCS). Other research has pointed to extremely limited consumption of prohibited drugs on the part of the elderly (Leitner et al., 1993).

• The 'contact sample' invited to tackle the drugs component numbered 11,244 people, aged 16–59. Of these, 304 declined to take part (2.7%, as compared with 2.5% for the 1994 BCS), leaving a baseline group totalling 10,940.

Other details about the 1996 BCS are:

• Interviews were mainly carried out between January and April 1996, by staff of Social & Community Planning Research (SCPR), equipped with laptop computers. For most of the interview – other than the drugs component – it was the interviewer who entered the answers given by respondents.

• The sample of households was drawn from the Small Users Postcode Address File, a listing of all postal delivery points. A stratified multi-stage random probability design was used to select addresses. There was planned over-sampling in inner-city postal sectors.

• Within households, final selection of one individual to be interviewed was randomised, no substitution being allowed. Where necessary, various callbacks were made by the interviewer.

• The response rate – at the level of individuals – was 82.5 per cent, which is extremely high for a national household survey of the general population.

• As is normal practice, the data obtained from the survey process were later adjusted or 'weighted', simply to ensure that households in different types of areas (such as inner cities) and individuals living in households of varying sizes all had fair and appropriate representation in the sample used for analysis.

One other important point needs to be made. As well as the core sample discussed above, which included ethnic minority interviewees roughly in line with their presence in the general population, an additional ethnic minority 'booster' sample was recruited. This was achieved in two ways. First, additional areas with a relatively high percentage of household heads from ethnic minorities were added to the sample. The second method was 'focused enumeration', for which addresses close to those selected for the core sample were also approached. The purpose of the booster sample was to provide sufficient numbers of ethnic minority respondents to carry out detailed statistical analysis. Further details of ethnic minority sampling and self-report processes are given elsewhere (Chapter 4 and Appendix C). It is important to emphasise that the booster sample is not deployed until Chapter 4 – the chapter in which ethnic comparisons are addressed.

Further details of the sampling and survey process are given elsewhere in this report: in Appendix A, in the case of the core sample. There is also a separate technical report (Hales and Stratford, 1997).

A society alive to drug misuse

It would be difficult to carry out a survey of drug misuse in the general population were it not for the fact that most people have quite a high level of knowledge about drug misuse. When respondents were asked which drugs they had heard of, by way of a warm-up exercise in the drugs self-report component, both young and old claimed impressive levels of awareness. It is perhaps unsurprising that over 90 per cent of those aged 16-29 had heard of cannabis, amphetamine, LSD, magic mushrooms, tranquillisers such as Valium and Temazepam, cocaine, crack, heroin and steroids. It is rather more striking that over 90 per cent of those aged 30-59 reckoned they had heard of all of those substances with the exception of magic mushrooms (see Table B.1, in Appendix B).

Levels of knowledge of the different types of drugs were nearly all as high or even slightly higher than in the 1994 BCS. The greatest increase in knowledge was of Methadone, widely used in the treatment of drug addicts. As many as 71 per cent had heard of it: a significant increase compared to the equivalent figure for the 1994 BCS of 66 per cent.

Confronted with the term Semeron, it is perhaps not altogether surprising that four per cent indicated that they had heard of this bogus substance: it has a plausible ring to it, after all. The relevant figure in the 1994 BCS was precisely the same.

High levels of knowledge do not necessarily imply high levels of use: far from it. But this brief discussion of the public's knowledge of different drugs does help to set the scene for the assessment of patterns of misuse, as presented in the next chapter.

2 Latest findings

Introduction

This chapter provides an up-to-date snapshot of patterns of drug misuse in England and Wales. The focus is solely on the findings of the 1996 BCS: the – relatively modest – change in the level of misuse, in comparison with the previous BCS, carried out in 1994, forms the subject of the next chapter.

What kinds of people do or do not try prohibited drugs, in terms of age, gender and other characteristics? Who consumes specific substances? To what extent are people taking not just one kind of drug but perhaps more than one, during the survey's various recall periods (ever/lifetime, last year, last month)? Who resorts to injection?

The final part of this chapter, building on more detailed analytical work carried out with the 1994 BCS, discusses a number of key characteristics that serve to differentiate users from non-users. These characteristics, all of them significantly associate with patterns of misuse, are themselves inter-related:

• alcohol consumption

• smoking

• health status

• household income

• employment status

• lifestyle: evenings out.

Starting point

First, Table 2.1 shows the prevalence of drug misuse over the three different recall periods, in terms of respondents' age groups and gender. The focus is on consumption of any drug whatsoever.

Table 2.1 Percentages of respondents who used drugs ever or in the last year or month, by age group and by gender

	16–19	20–24	25–29	30–39	40–59	All
Ever/lifetime						
Males	48	57	48	39	21	34
Females	42	43	35	26	13	24
Anybody	45	49	41	32	17	29
Last year						
Males	35	32	22	11	3	13
Females	27	23	13	6	2	8
Anybody	31	27	17	8	2	10
Last month						
Males	23	24	13	6	2	8
Females	15	12	7	3	1	4
Anybody	19	18	10	5	1	6

Note: Source: 1996 BCS (weighted data). A point to bear in mind throughout this chapter and the next is that the actual or unweighted number of people completing the drugs self-report component in the core sample for the full 16-59 age range is 10,940.

From one perspective, this table shows that consumption of prohibited drugs is relatively widespread: at least where ever/lifetime use is concerned, particularly on the part of those in the younger age groups. The highest such figure is that of 49 per cent, on the part of the 20-24 age group. Obviously the fact that virtually one in two young people in their early twenties have tried drugs gives cause for concern; it is also the kind of figure much hyped in the media. It is, however, important to bear in mind a broader context. Other survey research indicates that a very substantial minority of young people have committed non-drug crimes, involving violence or property or suchlike, at some point in their lives (Graham and Bowling, 1995).

Perhaps a more meaningful way of appraising the prevalence of drug misuse is to focus on the other two recall periods, the last year and the last month. This takes us much closer to people's everyday lives. Reported rates of drug consumption drop substantially as between ever and the last year, and then less steeply as between the last year and the last month. We know from other research that roughly three-quarters of last-month users can be deemed regular users (Parker et al., 1995). Clearly, when drug taking becomes a regular habit, dependency is more likely to develop. But numbers involved in last-month consumption are comparatively limited: less than one in five of the 16-19 and 20-24 age groups, dropping to one in ten of the 25-29 age group, and then down to one in twenty of the 30-39 age group. In other words, at least on the basis of this recent survey, regular or even semi-regular drug misuse is something that nearly everyone has grown out of by the time they are into their thirties. And, of course, in many cases, drugs towards the less damaging end of the spectrum are involved, rather than, say, heroin. Indeed, across all age groups, additional analysis indicates that a majority of last-month drug misusers have only consumed cannabis, rather than cannabis and any other drug, or just other drugs.

Continuing with Table 2.1, one other important aspect remains: the gender gap. Males are generally more likely to report drug taking than females. This gap widens to some extent as one switches from ever/lifetime to the last year and then to the last month. It also broadens from the youngest age group through to the oldest, irrespective of recall period. In other words, it is only in the youngest age group, and for the least sensitive recall period (ever), that the gap becomes close, running at a ratio of 1.1 to 1. Obviously, this gap is reminiscent of the – admittedly larger – male/female faultlines affecting crime and deviance more generally.

However, the remaining tables in this report are framed in terms of an undifferentiated 'anybody'. Readers will need to remember that males have somewhat higher rates than the androgynous anybody, and females rather lower ones. Those requiring greater detail should refer to the more detailed tables in the appendices.

Different drugs

Thinking about 'any' drug has obvious limitations. Equally, it would be cumbersome to look separately at all 17 substances. A good compromise is to focus in turn on some key drugs and then on groups of drugs.

We can start usefully with the two prohibited drugs most widely consumed, cannabis and amphetamine. Alongside them, we can consider two others that are widely perceived as especially damaging, both here and in other Western countries such as the United States: heroin and crack cocaine.

As shown by the top row of Table 2.2, cannabis is substantially more popular than any other prohibited drug. It has been tried by, very roughly, a third of those in the three age groups spanning 16 through to 29. No other drug even begins to approach this level of use. The next most popular substance is amphetamine, taken by, at most, half as many. Indeed, the same proportion of those aged 16–19 reports consumption of cannabis in the last month as has ever tried amphetamine (16%). Whatever its harmfulness to some or all users (Thomas, 1996), cannabis is unusual among the prohibited drugs in that it does not lend itself to injection; nor is its consumption associated with acquisitive crime on the part of dependent users. On these two grounds, the fact that consumption of cannabis is substantially more widespread than that of any other drug is of some importance.

Table 2.2 Percentages of respondents who used four different drugs ever or in the last year or month, by age group

	16–19	20–24	25–29	30–59	All
Cannabis					
Ever	35	42	32	17	22
Year	27	24	15	4	9
Month	16	16	8	2	5
Amphetamine					
Ever	16	21	12	6	9
Year	12	11	4	1	3
Month	5	6	2	*	1
Heroin					
Ever	1	1	*	1	1
Year	*	*	*	*	*
Month	0	*	*	*	*
Crack					
Ever	1	2	1	*	1
Year	*	*	*	*	*
Month	*	0	*	*	*

Note: Figures under 0.5 are shown as * and those with no respondents as 0 (a general convention in this report). Source: 1996 BCS (weighted data).

By way of contrast, heroin and crack cocaine are drugs that are far more obviously damaging, both to individual consumers and to society as a whole. They are not uncommonly injected, particularly in the case of dependent heroin users; and they are clearly implicated in high-volume acquisitive crime (Parker and Bottomley, 1996; Parker and Kirby, 1996). The lifestyles of heroin and crack misusers actually in the throes of full-blown addiction are apt to be so chaotic that such people may be under-represented in the survey, for instance because they were unavailable for interview if their household – if indeed they had one – was contacted by the survey company. This may partly explain the rows of asterisks, denoting figures below 0.5 per cent, for last year and last month use of both heroin and crack cocaine, as shown in Table 2.2. (Another possibility is that there was a particular reluctance to admit to recent as opposed to lifetime consumption.) Yet even allowing for some element of under-reporting, for these two especially damaging and stigmatised drugs, their use is undoubtedly confined to a very small minority, across the sample as a whole. One further point to bear in mind, drawing on additional analysis, is that there are some specific areas with higher – or lower – than average levels of heroin consumption. For instance, in the Midlands, in the 16–24 age group, two per cent of respondents reported that they had tried heroin at some time in their lives.

Consumption of crack cocaine seems now to be spreading alongside that of heroin in at least some cities (Parker and Bottomley, 1996). As they note, crack is a 'cooked' version of cocaine, producing small 'rocks' (crystals); it is a "new delivery system for cocaine which seems to produce greater cravings on the part of users than cocaine powder. It can be injected, but is more often smoked". The results of the 1996 BCS seem to suggest that consumption of crack, while only involving one per cent of respondents even on a lifetime basis, is not far out of line with that of heroin. However, this rests on the ever/lifetime findings; where the last year and the last month are concerned, the extremely low numbers point to the need for considerable caution. It is worth bearing in mind a recent study indicating that, in Leicester, while crack enjoys considerable popularity among polydrug misusers on an occasional basis, it is not actually consumed on the same regular footing as heroin and certain other drugs (Home Office, 1997). Of course, against this, the other study just mentioned (Parker and Bottomley, 1996) shows crack being regularly consumed alongside a repertoire of other drugs, in parts of Manchester. The BCS contributes a further piece to a much larger jigsaw, enhancing our understanding of the spread of crack cocaine on the part of the general public, while still leaving the wider puzzle less than complete.

Groups of drugs

Moving beyond individual drugs, a key question is the extent to which respondents have consumed any one or more of various different groups of drugs which can, for the sake of convenience, be grouped together. Two such sets are presented in Table 2.3. The first of these is *opiates+*, comprising heroin, methadone, cocaine and crack. While it is a social rather than a scientific or medical classification, it proved useful in presenting the results of the 1994 BCS. And recent research has confirmed both the importance and the overlap in consumption of these four drugs, where habitual misusers are concerned (Parker and Kirby, 1996). The second group of drugs, *hallucinants*, comprises various stimulants and hallucinogens, sometimes linked with dances, parties and raves, although in practice they may also be used in other settings (Power, 1995).

Starting with the opiates+ category, Table 2.3 shows that, within the younger age groups (16-19, 20-24, 25-29), the proportion of respondents that had ever used one or more of these drugs was between three per cent and seven per cent; reducing to between one per cent and two per cent for the last year; and then dropping to a consistent one per cent over the last month. While these are higher figures than for heroin (or crack) by itself, they still speak of the comparatively rare nature of such behaviour.

Table 2.3 Percentages of respondents who used two different sets of drugs (opiates+, hallucinants) ever or in the last year or month, by age group

	16-19	20-24	25-29	30-59	All
Opiates+					
Ever	3	7	4	3	3
Year	1	2	1	*	1
Month	1	1	1	*	*
Hallucinants					
Ever	27	30	22	9	14
Year	16	14	6	1	4
Month	7	7	3	1	2

Note: Hallucinants comprise amphetamine, LSD, magic mushrooms (psilocybin), ecstasy and poppers (amyl nitrite). Opiates+ comprise heroin, methadone, cocaine and crack, a grouping listed simply as opiates in the report on the 1994 BCS drugs findings. As presented throughout this report, methadone - used officially by way of a substitute drug in treating heroin addicts in particular – involves unprescribed use. Source: 1996 BCS (weighted data).

The hallucinants charted across the lower part of Table 2.3 have a wider following. The drugs in this group are amphetamine, LSD, magic mushrooms (psilocybin), ecstasy and poppers (amyl or butyl nitrite). One of these drugs – ecstasy – attracts heavy attention from the media, partly owing to a number of deaths in particularly poignant circumstances, but it is actually the least often consumed out of the five, if only by a narrow margin.

With the hallucinants, as with prohibited drugs in general, there are clear signs of a lessening in consumption by those in their late twenties, if not with a slightly younger age group. For instance, last-month consumption of hallucinants by those aged 25-29 stands at three per cent, as opposed to seven per cent for both 16-19 and 20-24 age groups. In the wider literature dealing both with drug misuse and other delinquent behaviour, this kind of transformation carries the tag of maturation reform theory (Elliott et al., 1989; Farrington, 1986; Kandel and Logan, 1984).

Consumption of numbers of different drugs

We have already seen how a majority of those reporting drug consumption in the last month restricted themselves to a single drug, cannabis. However, there are also some people whose repertoire is wider, perhaps amounting to polydrug misuse. In some cases, one drug is taken to counterbalance the effect of another, consumed previously or even at the same time.

So far as this survey of the general population is concerned, the picture that emerges is a mixed one. Table 2.4 is the first in a sequence differentiated, agewise, simply in terms of 16-29 and 30-59, besides the full age range (16-59). It shows that for young people on a lifetime basis, the various groups consuming two, or even more than two, prohibited substances outnumber those who have confined themselves to just one. To be more specific, a total of 26 per cent had taken upwards of two different drugs, as opposed to 19 per cent who had only ever tried one kind. On the other hand, consumption of large numbers of drugs (10+), even by young people on a lifetime basis, is extremely rare, running at no more than one per cent. And it is also worth remembering that, as shown by the first column of figures from the left, the majority even of those aged 16-29 are in the 'no drug' category.

Table 2.4 Percentages of respondents in different age groups who used varying numbers of different drugs ever or in the last year or month

	No drug	One drug	Two drugs	3-9 drugs	10+ drugs	**Total**
Ever						
16-29	55	19	9	16	1	100
30-59	78	13	4	5	*	100
All	71	15	6	8	*	100
Last year						
16-29	76	14	5	6	*	100
30-59	96	4	1	*	*	100
All	90	7	2	2	*	100
Last month						
16-29	85	10	3	2	0	100
30-59	98	2	*	*	*	100
All	94	4	1	1	*	100

Note: Source: 1996 BCS (weighted data). The maximum number of drugs which could have been reported was 17, but this would have included Semeron, the fictitious drug, which was reported by merely a handful of all 10,940 respondents: five ever, two for the last year, one for the last month.

While on a lifetime basis the use of more than one different drug is not particularly unusual on the part of young people, a rather different pattern characterises their more recent drug misuse, and also that of older respondents, irrespective of the recall period. From all these other perspectives, consumption of more than one drug is less prevalent than consumption of just one substance. And, of course, the vast majority of all respondents are in the 'no drug' category.

Given that the last-month findings come closest to reflecting people's daily lives, this aspect is probably of greatest importance in understanding the use of different drugs. Only ten per cent of all those aged 16-29 have taken a single type of drug in the last month; no more than five per cent have consumed between two and nine drugs; and none whatsoever have taken upwards of ten. Drug misuse is as much a matter of custom and habit as most other social activities.

Injecting of drugs

If consumption of a wide range of drugs is far from commonplace, injection of drugs is even rarer. An extra question was added to the 1996 BCS, to shed some light on the extent to which drug misusers were resorting to injection. It was only asked of those who reported consumption of drugs in the last year, from within a wide range of substances. With fuller information in Appendix D, just some key details are needed here. Injecting use was reported by three per cent of the relevant group of last-year misusers: equivalent to 0.1 per cent of the full sample aged 16–59. This figure of three per cent is broadly in line with an obvious point of comparison, the Four Cities Survey (although there the question concerned injecting ever). As the authors of that survey point out, household surveys do not necessarily reveal the full extent of injecting, precisely because it is sometimes associated with chaotic lives (Leitner et al., 1993). The format of the BCS question on injecting did not pinpoint which drugs were being injected. It is however possible to assess the characteristics of the injectors: they were predominately white males of relatively low socio-economic status, whose age was on average around the mid 30s.

Drinking, smoking and health as explanatory factors

The report on the 1994 BCS showed that certain health-related factors were strongly associated with drug misuse, as were socio-economic and lifestyle ones. The remainder of this chapter presents key findings across this range of issues. We start with the links between drug misuse and respondents' drinking, smoking and general health status. With the drug misuse, our focus is on last-year consumption, given that this is the second in a series of biennial reports where there is, inevitably, particular interest in last-year findings, which are appropriately up to date.

Heavy drinking in particular is a very strong predictor of drug misuse, or so the equivalent report on the 1994 BCS showed (Ramsay and Percy, 1996). We know from other research that smoking can also be a sign of drug misuse (Leitner et al., 1993); accordingly a question was added to the 1996 BCS, the first time that this survey has covered smoking. Finally, being in poor health is associated – although not so strongly or consistently – with drug misuse. These three variables, which are obviously inter-related, are all brought together in Table 2.5. In fact only the health variable is absolutely identical to that used in the 1994 BCS. The one on drinking alcohol was revised to bring it into line with the approach followed in, for instance, the General Household Survey (Smith and Browne, 1992). This involves a two-part format in which respondents are asked, first, how often on average they consume alcohol (against a specific scale) and, secondly, about the amount usually consumed; levels of consumption can be calculated from combined responses. Each of the variables, concerning drinking, smoking and health, is subdivided into a pair of contrasting categories. As displayed in Table 2.5, the upper category of each pair (light/no drinking, no smoking, better health) is characterised by less high levels of drug misuse than the lower category (heavy drinking, smoking, poorer health), virtually regardless of age group.

Table 2.5 Percentages of respondents who used drugs in the last year, in terms of drinking levels, smoking and health status, by age group

	16–29	30–59	All
Drinking			
Light/none	15	3	7
Heavier	39	7	18
Smoking			
Non-smokers	15	3	6
Smokers	40	8	19
Health status			
Better	23	4	10
Poorer	32	6	13

Note: Source: 1996 BCS (weighted data). Within the **drinking** category, the heavier category drinks upwards of one unit a day, the light/no category drinks less than that (or none). The former category comprises 33%; the latter, 67% of the total eligible population. Within the **smoking** category, non-smokers acount for 68% of this population; smokers, 32%. Within the **health** field, those in poorer health (assessing themselves as in fair, bad, or very bad health) accounted for 18%; those in better health (assessing themselves in good or very good health) accounted for 82%. Since the drinking and smoking findings are based on partly or wholly new questions (and are of some importance), more detailed tables are provided in Appendix B, as Tables B5 and B6.

The contrasts within the drinking and smoking pairs of categories are particularly sharp. Both heavier drinkers and the smokers have drugs prevalence rates between two and three times those of respectively, lighter/none drinkers and non–smokers (there is of course an overlap between the groups categorised as heavier drinkers and smokers). Links of this kind, particularly between drinking and drug misuse, have been noted in other recent research, including an article which argues that young people, at least in the North West, are tending increasingly to consume both alcohol and prohibited drugs as a 'big bang', or maximum-impact binge (Measham, 1996). That article also notes that there are instances of particular brands of alcohol being marketed or packaged in ways that mirror prohibited drugs.

An association between smoking and drug misuse has also been noted in other recent research (Leitner et al., 1993; Miller and Plant, 1996). The added advantage of the BCS, even with merely a simple question on current use ("Do you smoke cigarettes, cigars or a pipe nowadays?") lies in its extremely large national sample, embracing a wide age range. One obvious factor is that cannabis, the prohibited drug most widely consumed, is normally smoked; it can be mixed with tobacco. As with the alcohol/drugs association documented both in this BCS drugs report and its predecessor, the links between smoking and drug misuse pose interesting questions for the optimum framing of drugs policy.

The association between drug misuse and respondents' health is a complicated one, not yet fully understood (Moore and Polsgrove, 1991). What is clear, both from the 1994 and 1996 BCS, is that those who reckon themselves to be in relatively good health report lower levels of drug misuse; here, however, the contrast is not so sharp as between smokers/non-smokers or between heavier drinkers and lighter/no drinkers, especially with those aged 30+.

Looking at the health-related findings alongside those on drinking and smoking, there is clearly scope for promoting drugs prevention within a broader framework of healthy living, itself a quintessential late-twentieth century concern. Of course, this is only one such positive context, albeit an important one. Household income, employment status and lifestyle are also influential, if complicating, factors in accounting for drug misuse, as the remainder of this chapter confirms.

The socio-economic dimension: income and employment status

The social structure, exemplified here by household income and individual employment status, has its own subtle but important effect on patterns of drug misuse. Obviously there is some interaction with health-related variables; it is well established that the highest proportion of smokers is to be found among the poorer social groups (Smith and Browne, 1992). Drinking, however, is not socially stratified in the same way. If anything, on account of the high cost of purchasing large amounts of alcohol, the pattern is an inverse one, as has been consistently shown by the same source, the General Household Survey. In terms of prevalence patterns, drug misuse is both similar to, yet different from, other – legally acceptable - drug taking. It is worth bearing in mind that it can be cheaper to get 'out of one's head' with some prohibited drugs than with alcohol (Ramsay, 1994a).

If some people think of drug misusers as poverty-stricken denizens of inner-city areas, this is an exaggerated assessment. On the contrary, drug misuse in general is spread relatively evenly across all social groups, manual and non-manual, inner-city and suburban, rich and poor (Ramsay and Percy, 1996). Of course, drug misuse may be more visible in certain inner-city areas; areas which do indeed have more than their share of especially damaging forms of misuse (Leitner et al., 1993).

While different levels of drinking or smoking or even variations in health were associated with correspondingly neatly graded levels of drug misuse – making possible the highly simplified format of Table 2.5 – a potentially flexible socio-economic variable like income does not lend itself to the same schematic presentation in terms of drug misuse. Those in the very poorest group, living in households with an income of under £5,000, have higher rates of drug misuse than other groups, but they are scarcely much above average. Essentially, Table 2.6 shows that, by itself, income is not a powerful differentiator in terms of drug misuse.

Table 2.6 Percentages of respondents in households with varying levels of income who used drugs in the last year, by age group

	16–29 age group	30–59 age group	All
Under £5,000	26	6	14
£5,000–14,999	21	6	10
£15,000–29,999	22	4	9
£30,000+	23	5	9
AVERAGE	24	4	10

Note: In preparing this table, respondents answering don't know/refused have been excluded (they comprised 7%). The original proportion of respondents in each category was as follows: under £5k, nine per cent; £5k to under £15k, 24 per cent; £15k to under £30k, 38 per cent; upwards of £30k, 22 per cent. Source: 1996 BCS (weighted data).

While low income is a modest pointer to drug misuse in general, Table 2.7 shows that not having a job is at least as important a factor, if only in the case of the 16–29 age group. This table serves as a convenient starting point for a discussion of links between drug misuse and employment status.

Table 2.7 Percentages of respondents of differing employment status who used drugs in the last year, by age group

	16–29	30–59	All
Employed full-time	22	5	9
Not employed	27	5	13

Note: Part-time employees (15% of those aged 16–29; 19% of 30–59s; 18% of all) have been excluded from this table, so as to keep it as simple as possible. Within the 16–29 age group as discussed below, 67 per cent were in work, either full or part-time; seven per cent were waiting/looking for work (unemployed); one per cent were sick; 16 per cent were students, living in non-institutional settings accessible to interviewers; nine per cent were home-makers; and one per cent others. Source:1996 BCS (weighted data).

To be more specific, Table 2.7 indicates a contrast, on the part of the 16–29 age group, between the prevalence rates of those not in paid employment, at 27 per cent, and those with full-time jobs, at 22 per cent. This contrast was substantially sharper for one particular subgroup, those unemployed. As many as 45 per cent of unemployed people in the 16–29 age group reported drug use within the last year, which counts as a highly significant finding.

Socio-economic strains and stresses, notably unemployment, do make a difference to drug prevalence patterns, but are still only part of a wider picture. There are also other kinds of pressure or influence, with which the rest of this chapter is concerned, which can be summed up in the one word: lifestyles.

Lifestyle: evenings out

To be young may or may not be heaven any more. In fact, recent research suggests that young people are exposed to a wide range of pressures, from their peer group as well as from socio-economic forces: pressures which, while they are perhaps relieved in some ways by 'youth culture', are also intensified by its very existence (Rutter and Smith, 1995). It certainly makes good sense, in looking at lifestyles, to focus specifically on the 16–29 age group. Young people in their late teens and twenties have, as we have seen, relatively high rates of drug misuse, especially on a lifetime basis. It is also relevant that, in the 1990s, young people have tended not to leave home and establish a fully independent existence until they are in their mid or in some cases late twenties (Graham and Bowling, 1995; Rutter and Smith, 1995). The 16–29 age group is distinctive as never before. As many as 63 per cent of BCS respondents in this age range were single rather than married or cohabiting (or widowed or divorced). One final point by way of introduction about lifestyles is that they reflect both personal choices and the diffferential availability of prohibited drugs in various settings. For instance, drugs are more likely to be offered or purchased in pubs than places of worship; the extent to which young people decide to frequent one or the other could make a difference.

Irrespective of what young people do when they go out in the evening, the very fact of their going out is associated – to some degree – with an increased likelihood of drug misuse. In a sense, this is unsurprising. Previous research has shown that social isolation is a protective factor where delinquency in general is concerned (Farrington, 1995). In addition, there may well be links between going out and drinking (perhaps also with smoking), the importance of which has been discussed earlier in this chapter. The top part of Table 2.8 shows that there is a significant contrast in drugs prevalence rates for the last year between, on the one hand, those who went out for three or more evenings in the last week (at 32%); and, on the other, those who only went out once or twice, or not at all (at 17%). This is a particularly telling contrast, in that young people were fairly evenly divided between those who went out for upwards of three nights in the last week, and less than that.

Going out in the evening brings us back to the matter of alcohol. Visiting a pub is not quite so revealing an indicator as heavy consumption of alcohol, not least because the vast majority of young people (80%) went out to a pub, club or bar during the last month. Nonetheless, the minority who did not do so clearly had a strikingly low rate of drug misuse (10%), as shown by the lower part of Table 2.8

Table 2.8 Percentages of young people (16–29) who used drugs in the last year, in terms of their number of evenings outside the home during the previous week, and visits to pubs/clubs/bars in previous month

	Percentage of young people using drugs in last year
Evenings out in previous week	
None, or no more than two	17
Between three and seven/all	32
Visits to pub/club/bar in previous month	
None	10
One or more	28
AVERAGE FOR ALL YOUNG PEOPLE	24

Note: Within this 16-29 age group, 46 per cent went out between 3 and 7 nights a week; 44 per cent went out only once or twice, or not at all. Pubs/bars/clubs were visited by 80 per cent, within the last month. Source: 1996 BCS (weighted data).

Lifestyle is undoubtedly important in understanding patterns of drug misuse. In the last resort, however, it resembles all the various other factors discussed in this chapter, in that it only offers a partial explanation. A final dimension which reinforces this point emerges from patterns of answers to another lifestyle question, this time one asking what respondents did the last time they went out in the evening. Those mentioning going to a pub, or else a dance/party/disco, had the highest rates of last-year misuse (33% and 34% respectively). But that still leaves roughly two-thirds of those with relatively risky options for their last night out as non-users, so far as the last year is concerned.

Conclusion

In this chapter, we have explored various major contours of drug misuse. At some point in their lives, 45 per cent of young people aged 16–29 have taken prohibited drugs, yet misuse within the last year or month is far less widespread, at 24 per cent and 15 per cent respectively. And over half of young, last-month drug misusers have only consumed one substance, cannabis.

Drinking and smoking patterns are strongly linked with drug misuse, together with some socio-economic factors, notably employment status. If, in this chapter, the socio-economic factors do not necessarily seem to be particularly influential, it is worth remembering that we have not considered different subgroups within the 16–29 age bracket. We know that the socio-economic dimension weighs more heavily with the 20–29 age group than with those still in their teens, as was documented in the longer and more detailed report on the previous BCS (Ramsay and Percy, 1996).

This broad overview closed with an assessment of lifestyle factors among 16–29s. For them, 'getting a life', in the sense of going out a lot in the evening, is associated with above-average levels of drug misuse. But there remains a need for caution, here as with other factors. As many as two-thirds of those young people whose last night out was the relatively 'risky' choice of visiting a pub or club had not consumed a prohibited drug within the last year. Drug taking is a multi-causal phenomenon, for which no individual factor offers an overriding explanation.

3 Changing times?

Introduction

Surveys, once repeated, can be particularly useful in helping us to understand any change over time. Since the early 1980s, successive findings from the main component of the BCS – concerned with victimisation – have formed an increasingly important indicator, alongside the recorded crime statistics, of changing levels of victimisation experienced by members of the public. Now that a drugs self-report component has been added, following the very same format for both the 1994 and the 1996 BCS, a drug misuse time series is beginning to emerge. Like the much longer-runnning 'National Household Survey on Drug Abuse' in the United States, this should become a vital means of keeping track of changing patterns of drug misuse in England and Wales. But these are still early days; with only two sets of findings for comparison, any interpretation of trends can only be provisional.

Crucial indicator: consumption of drugs within the last year

The drugs self-report component of the BCS has three recall periods: ever/lifetime, the last year and the last month. All three have some potential relevance in understanding change over time. However, self-reported drug taking within the last year is particularly crucial. Whereas ever/lifetime use may or may not involve consumption within the two-year time period since the previous BCS, last-year use is obviously well clear of that particular complication. Moreover, consumption of drugs within the last year is reported by a significantly larger group of respondents than last-month consumption; this means that changes in drug taking over the last year tend to emerge more clearly. Nevertheless, shifts in drug misuse on both a lifetime and a last-month footing are also discussed, briefly, later in this chapter.

Table 3.1 charts consumption of individual drug types in the last year, and also the use of any drug over the same period, for both the 16–29 age group and the full sample (16–59), as found in both the 1994 and 1996 BCS.

Table 3.1 Percentages of respondents in the 1994 and 1996 BCS who used different drugs during the last year, by age group

	16–29 age group		16–59 age group	
	1994 BCS	1996 BCS	1994 BCS	1996 BCS
Cannabis	20	21	8	9
Amphetamine	7	8	2	3
LSD	4	3	1	1
Magic mushroom	3	2	1	1
Smoke unknown	2	1	1	1
Ecstasy	3	4	1	1
Poppers	4	3	1	1
Tranquillisers	1	1	1	*
Glue, gas, etc.	1	*	*	*
Cocaine	1	1	*	1
Pills unknown	1	*	*	*
Crack	*	*	*	*
Methadone	*	*	*	*
Heroin	*	*	*	*
Steroids	*	*	*	*
Semeron	0	0	*	*
Anything else	*	*	*	*
ANY DRUG	23	24	10	10

Note: Sources: 1994 and 1996 BCS (weighted data). None of the changes for different drugs as between the 1994 and 1996 surveys are statistically significant: that is, they are no greater than those that could be generated by sampling error.

It is clear, first, for the full 16–59 age range, that there is no change from the 1994 to the 1996 BCS, with figures for any drug staying constant at 10 per cent. From a statistical perspective, the same is true of the all-important 16-29 age group. Relevant figues for different kinds of drugs either remain the same from one sweep of the BCS to the next or are no more than one percentage point different: these changes are not statistically significant. That also holds true for any drug: the increase for the 16-29 age group, from 23 per cent to 24 per cent, is a very modest one, which is not statistically significant. Even with large social surveys, only relatively substantial behavioural changes emerge as significant - highlighting the need to wait for the results of the 1998 BCS, for clarification as to what is happening.

Given the importance of the 16-29 age group, which is more obviously 'at risk', especially its younger members, we need to inspect for any divergences within that age range. Table 3.2 shows a small decrease for the 16-19 age group, coupled with modest increases for the 20-24 and 25-29 age groups. None of these three changes attains statistical significance. (A note at the bottom of Table 3.2 provides further detail.)

Table 3.2 Percentages of respondents in the 1994 and 1996 BCS who used any drug during the last year, within the 16–29 age range

	1994 BCS	1996 BCS
Age group		
16–19 subgroup	34	31
20–24 subgroup	25	27
25–29 subgroup	15	17
16–29 AGE RANGE	23	24

Note: Sources: 1994 and 1996 BCS (weighted data). None of the changes between equivalent groups in these two sweeps of the BCS is statistically significant (that is, within a 5% or even a 10% parameter as measured by Z scores, using a two-tailed test and allowing for a design effect of 1.2). For the 16–29 age range as a whole, unweighted numbers of respondents were 2,777 in the 1994 BCS and 3,029 in the 1996 BCS.

It is also possible to focus on drug misuse by people of different ages, that is, to look separately at those aged 16, 17 and so forth. In each sweep of the BCS, the total number of relevant respondents reduces to little more than 150 in each year group, for the more 'at risk' category aged 16-24. For that reason, the relevant table is only presented in the appendices, as Table B.7. It shows that while figures for consumption of any drug within the last year, by those aged 17, 18 and 19, were lower in the 1996 BCS than in the 1994 BCS, equivalent figures for those aged 16 increased (reaching the highest level for any age group). Given that numbers are so limited, all that can safely be concluded is that there is no sign that drug misuse is tailing off on the part of those in their late teens. Or, in other words, the general picture so far, among the very youngest respondents as among those in their twenties, suggests relatively stable levels of drug misuse.

Lifetime and last-month consumption of drugs

The ever/lifetime and last-month perspectives, while less instructive than the last year, still help to complete the picture. Focusing on the 16–29 age range and its three subgroups, consumption just of any drug is presented in Table 3.3. The overall pattern is clearly reminiscent of the previous table (3.2).

Table 3.3 Percentages of respondents in the 1994 and 1996 BCS who used any drug, ever or during the last month, within the 16–29 age range

	Used ever/lifetime		Used last month	
	1994 BCS	1996 BCS	1994 BCS	1996 BCS
Age group				
16–19 subgroup	46	45	20	19
20–24 subgroup	44	49	15	18
25–29 subgroup	39	41	9	10
All in 16–29 age range	43	45	14	15

Note: Sources: 1994 and 1996 BCS (weighted data). On an ever/lifetime footing, the various changes between equivalent groups in these two sweeps of the BCS are not statistically significant, with the limited exception of the 20–24 age group where, using a two-tailed test, the ten per cent parameter is reached, with a Z score incorporating a design effect of 1.2. The last-month changes are not significant, using the same criteria.

Both the ever/lifetime and the last-month pairs of columns repeat the now familiar pattern of a slight increase in consumption as between the 1994 and 1996 BCS on the part of the full set of respondents aged 16–29; coupled with a modest drop on the part of the 16–19 age group and equally modest increases for the other two subgroups. The largest increase, the only one which is significant, occurs on an ever/lifetime basis, with the 20–24 age group (up from 44% to 49%; see note below Table 3.3). However, precisely because of the long recall period – with its implication that, for some respondents, drug use might only have happened more than two years before – such a finding does not necessarily reflect appreciable change from one sweep of the BCS to the next.

The last-month aspect confirms the general pattern, with no statistically significant changes. There is a small increase for the 16–29 age group as a whole (up from 14% to 15%), and only subtle shifts over time as between the three subgroups.

No one could conclude that consumption of prohibited drugs is dropping across England and Wales as a whole, on the part of the 16–29 age group. It is equally clear, on the basis of findings for all three recall periods, that any increases are, almost without exception, non-significant, even when looking separately at all three smaller age bands.

Regional variation

Although a general picture of relative stability has just been painted for the country as a whole, it is in some respects an artificial one. It certainly masks regional variation in levels of drug misuse, which at least to some extent reaches statistical significance. The report on the 1994 BCS noted that Greater London had the highest prevalence rates, for younger and older respondents alike, and for different recall periods (Ramsay and Percy, 1996). With the 1996 BCS, however, London's distinctive status shows signs of being eroded, especially with the younger age groups.

It is not altogether surprising that the gap between the North (or the North and the Midlands) and Greater London and perhaps its southern hinterland seems to be narrrowing. An important longitudinal study of young people in Liverpool and Manchester has consistently revealed high rates of drug misuse (Parker et al., 1995). Given the association between alcohol and prohibited drugs, discussed in the previous chapter, it is also highly relevant that the North (including the North West, with Manchester and Liverpool as leading conurbations) has a tradition of heavy drinking in comparison with other regions (Smith and Browne, 1992). On a more subtle note, Manchester's pre-eminence in terms of clubs and music for youth markets could conceivably be worth bearing in mind, not least with 'hallucinants' or dance drugs. Drug misuse, perhaps especially in terms of change on a regional footing, can be affected by 'fashion' or demand, as well as changes in supply/availability.

This change in regional patterns of drug misuse is best understood by focusing just on the 16–29 age group from, once again, a last-year perspective. Table 3.4, which has pairs of columns charting, respectively, use of any drug and use of hallucinants or dance drugs (amphetamine, LSD, magic mushrooms, ecstasy and poppers), in the two sweeps of the BCS, provides our introduction to the regional shift.

Focusing first on last-year use of any drug, Table 3.4 shows at least a slight overall narrowing of last-year prevalence rates, between some of the major northern and southern regions. The reduction in London and the increases in the Midlands and the North are all non-significant when assessed individually. However, as discussed in the note accompanying Table 3.4, the increases in the Midlands and the North, taken together as a single enlarged area, are statistically significant.

Table 3.4 Percentages of respondents aged 16–29 in the 1994 and 1996 BCS who used any drug or 'hallucinants' in the last year, by region

	Used any drug in last year		Used hallucinants in last year	
	1994 BCS	1996 BCS	1994 BCS	1996 BCS
Region				
North	22	26	11	14
Midlands	16	19	9	11
Anglia	22	22	9	8
Wales	27	15	9	10
South	25	26	10	10
London	32	29	13	9
ENGLAND/WALES	23	24	11	11

Note: Sources: 1994 and 1996 BCS (weighted data). Few individual changes are statistically significant, using a two-tailed test, with Z scores incorporating a design effect of 1.2. The reduction in Wales for any drug is significant (10% and 5% criteria), but is not matched by any reduction for hallucinants; a conjunction that could reflect local variation, within a region only containing around one-twentieth of the population of England and Wales. Also, given that Welsh 16-29 figures for any drug ever only fell slightly from one BCS to the next (from 44% to 40%), it is just possible that short-term cannabis 'droughts' could have had some limited effect; their existence is mentioned in the literature (ISDD, 1997). If the Midlands/North are aggregated, there are appreciable differences both for any drug (up from 20% to 23% between 1994 and 1996 BCS) and for hallucinants (up from 10% to 13%). These two differences are each statistically significant (10% criterion, other aspects as mentioned above).

These six regions are a condensed set of the nine standard English (or Welsh) regions, assembled as follows: London = Greater London (14% of respondents aged 16-29); South = SE + SW (32%); Wales = Wales (5%); Anglia = E Anglia (5%); Midlands = East + West Midlands (18%); North = North + Yorks/Humber + North West (27%).

Turning to the hallucinants or dance drugs on the right side of Table 3.4, a very similar pattern emerges. Focusing first on individual regions, there is a slight decrease in London, coupled with equally modest increases in the Midlands and the North. However, the increase for the combined Midlands/North is a significant one.

The suggestion that drug misuse may be increasing in the Midlands/North, but not London (or perhaps the South) is reinforced if one looks more closely at the very youngest group, comprising those aged 16–19, which can be seen as, potentially, a trend-setting cohort. Details are illustrated in Table 3.5. It is worth bearing in mind that total numbers are low, for this age group: less than 600 in each sweep of the BCS.

Table 3.5 Percentages of respondents aged 16–19 in the 1994 and 1996 BCS who used any drug or 'hallucinants' in the last year, by region

	Used any drug in last year		Used hallucinants in last year	
	1994 BCS	1996 BCS	1994 BCS	1996 BCS
Region				
North	31	35	17	22
Midlands	24	30	13	17
Anglia	41	28	21	8
Wales	37	19	14	12
South	39	32	20	13
London	45	29	26	13
ENGLAND/WALES	34	31	18	16

Note: Sources: 1994 and 1996 BCS (weighted data). Total numbers for the 16-19 age group were 538 and 580 in the 1994 and 1996 sweeps of the BCS respectively. Among the individual regions, the only statistically significant differences are in London, both for any drug and hallucinants; in each case the 10% criterion is met (usual two-tailed test). When the Midlands and North are combined, this gives 1994 and 1996 figures of 28 per cent and 33 per cent for any drug, and 15 per cent and 20 per cent for hallucinants; but the resulting differences over time are not significant, using the same ten per cent criterion.

Table 3.5 shows a significant reduction in drug misuse in London, even in terms of any drug (falling from 45% to 29%). And where the hallucinants or dance drugs are concerned, London's prevalence rate is halved (dropping from 26% to 13%). While other changes are not significant, it is interesting that – for this 16-19 age group – the North ends up with the highest rates of all the regions, both for any drug and for the hallucinants; when, in the 1994 BCS, its ranking was in each case a below-average one.

Conclusion

We have seen, in this chapter, how drug misuse as reported by young people aged 16-29 on a last-year footing – the best point of comparison – has been relatively stable across England and Wales. That is the main finding from this comparative analysis of self-reported drug misuse, from the 1994 and 1996 BCS. Closer inspection of the national data, on a regional basis, has shown some important variation, particularly in regional terms. While ethnicity and the ACORN housing classification have yet to be discussed – in the next chapter – none of the other social variables that we have been examining has such a coherent story of change to impart as the regional dimension. It is of course possible that, as more sweeps of the BCS are carried out in future, other elements of variation will start to emerge more clearly.

Specific findings from this pair of comparable national surveys can be summarised as follows:

- there was a very small increase in last-year use of any drug among those aged 16-29 (up from 23% to 24%, not a statistically significant change); while there was no change for the full age range of 16 to 59 (see Table 3.1)

- there were some fluctuations within the 16-29 age group, with a non-significant drop in last-year consumption of any drug on the part of those aged 16-19; coupled with a statistically significant increase on the part of those aged 20-24 (see Table 3.2)

- overall, for the crucial 16-29 age group as a whole, the picture is one of relatively constant consumption of prohibited drugs in general, whether on a lifetime, last year or last month footing. None of these three sets of indicators actually fell as between the 1994 and 1996 BCS (all increased non-significantly).

There was some interesting variation among the regions:

- for the important 16-29 age range, there was a significant increase in last-year consumption of any drug in the combined Midlands/North (see Table 3.4)

- drugs consumption in London, on a last-year footing, seems to have fallen at least slightly for the 16–29 age range. For those aged 16–19, the drop was a significant one (see Tables 3.4 and 3.5)

- In the 1994 BCS, London consistently had the highest level of drug misuse. However, in the 1996 BCS, if only for the 16–19 age group, it lost this ranking in favour of the North, for last-year consumption of both hallucinants and any drug.

All of these trends should become clearer when the 1998 BCS is carried out.

4 ACORN and ethnicity

Introduction

This chapter concerns two additional socio-economic aspects: housing areas (ACORN) and ethnicity. Each is important in a different way; each needs some assessment in its own right. Our main focus here is on the 1996 findings, but brief consideration of change is also offered.

ACORN

ACORN or – to spell it out in full – A Classification of Residential Neighbourhoods, is a system of grading households according to demographic, employment and housing features of the immediate locality. Developed as a market research tool, it can also be helpful for social research. The 1994 BCS report equivalent to this showed that ACORN offered some important insights into patterns of drug misuse, even though it was best examined in isolation from other socio-economic variables, of which it is a complex amalgam (Ramsay and Percy, 1996). It is available in different formats, two of which are presented here: a relatively simple configuration with six aspects and a more detailed one with 17.

Table 4.1 illustrates an ACORN continuum ranging literally from the top (the Thriving group, most prosperous of all) down to – at the bottom – the hard-pressed Striving group. As in much of the previous chapter, drug misuse means last-year consumption of any drug, on the part of 16–29, 30–59 and 16–59 age ranges.

Table 4.1 Percentages of respondents in 1996 BCS in neighbourhoods with different ACORN classsifications who used drugs in the last year, by age group

	16–29 age group	30–59 age group	16–59 (all)
ACORN category			
Thriving	27	2	8
Expanding	18	3	7
Rising	32	13	20
Settling	21	4	9
Aspiring	24	4	10
Striving	24	7	13
AVERAGE	24	4	10

Note: Source: 1996 BCS (weighted data). The proportion of respondents in each of these categories was as follows: Thriving, 21 per cent; Expanding, 12 per cent; Rising, eight per cent; Settling, 27 per cent; Aspiring, 14 per cent; Striving, 18 per cent.

This table shows that, irrespective of age group, the Rising category has the highest prevalence of all six categories. Who is in this Rising group? While not especially wealthy, it comprises people typically on their way up in society: hence the name. The designated subcategories under the Rising banner are 'affluent urbanites', 'prosperous professionals in metropolitan areas' and 'better-off executives in inner-city areas'. According to the *ACORN User Guide* (CACI, 1993), these are relatively adventurous people, who tend to have active leisure lives, going out in the evenings, visiting restaurants that serve exotic cuisine from round the world and consciously opting for holidays off the beaten track. Some undoubtedly swell the ranks of the "clubbing class", or so the report on the 1994 BCS drugs component suggested (Ramsay and Percy, 1996).

After the Rising group, that with the next-highest level of drug misuse varies as between different age bands, in a way that echoes socio-economic aspects discussed in the previous chapter. Within the 16–29 age range, the wealthy Thriving set has the next highest level of drug misuse after the Rising category, at 27 per cent as compared to the 32 per cent of the Rising group.

Yet within the 30–59 age group, and the full age range, the poorest group (Striving) follows next after the Rising one. Once past the age of 30, the Thriving group drops to a below-average prevalence level. For these prosperous people, drugs are a youthful indulgence, generally discarded as they grow older, whereas for the hard-pressed Striving group, drug misuse becomes proportionally more salient among its older members.

The ACORN findings of the 1996 BCS are broadly similar to those of the 1994 survey. Still focusing on last-year consumption, but only by the full age range and the more at-risk younger group (16–29), Table 4.2 indicates considerable consistency from one sweep of the BCS to the next. Some modest changes are apparent, at least for the 16–29 age range, but none are statistically significant (see note below table). With the full 16–59 age range, the figures are almost exactly the same in both sweeps of the BCS.

Table 4.2 Percentages of respondents in the 1994 and 1996 BCS in neighbourhoods with different ACORN classifications who have used drugs in the last year, by age group

	16–29 age group		16–59 age group	
	1994 BCS	1996 BCS	1994 BCS	1996 BCS
Thriving	22	27	7	8
Expanding	19	18	6	7
Rising	40	32	22	20
Settling	20	21	8	9
Aspiring	25	24	11	10
Striving	21	24	12	13
AVERAGE	23	24	10	10

Note: Source: 1994 and 1996 BCS (weighted data). None of these changes are statistically significant, in terms of two-tailed tests, allowing for a design effect of 1.2, on a five per cent or even a ten per cent probability basis; It is worth bearing in mind that the Rising group is the smallest of the six (see note below previous table).

It is also illuminating to focus on the subcategories within each of the six basic ACORN groups. The relatively limited change between the 1994 and 1996 sweeps of the BCS (as shown in Table 4.2) makes this a viable proposition. The more detailed ACORN format presented in Table 4.3 has a total of 17 classifications. Some interesting variation emerges. Within the Striving category, council estate residents in the 16–29 age group in areas of high unemployment have drugs prevalence rates for the last year that are consistently higher than those of the other four Striving sub-categories. Indeed, prevalence rates for these young people from high-unemployment/council areas match those of two out of three Rising sub-categories (and all three Thriving classifications), but they do not attain the same level as better-off executives in the inner-city. That last element of the Rising group has the highest level of any of the 17 subcategories, not just for the 16-29 age group but also for the full 16–59 age range.

Table 4.3 Percentages of respondents in the combined 1994/1996 BCS in neighbourhoods with different ACORN classifications who used drugs in the last year, by age group

	16-29 age group	16-59 (all)
Thriving		
Wealthy achievers, suburban areas	26	8
Affluent greys, rural communities	19	6
Prosperous pensioners, retirement areas	22	8
Expanding		
Affluent executives, family areas	20	7
Well-off workers, family areas	18	6
Rising		
Affluent urbanites, town & country areas	33	17
Prosperous professionals, metropolitan areas	33	18
Better-off executives, inner-city areas	39	26
Settling		
Comfortable middle-agers, mature home-owning areas	22	8
Skilled workers, home-owning areas	19	9
Aspiring		
New home owners, mature communities	23	9
White-collar workers, better-off multi-ethnic areas	27	13
Striving		
Older people, less prosperous areas	23	11
Council estate residents, better-off homes	20	11
Council estate residents, high unemployment	33	19
Council estate residents, greatest hardship	21	12
People in multi-ethnic, low-income areas	27	16
AVERAGE	24	10

Note: Source: 1994/1996 BCS, combined data sets, weighted. Unweighted N = 20,586. These categories refer to types of areas (and all who live in them, whatever their age group), not simply those actually mentioned in the various classifications, such as older people in less prosperous areas.

The more detailed ACORN classification includes a multi-ethnic aspect, involving two of the 17 sub-categories. Prevalence rates in those areas are above-average, running at 27 per cent in both cases. However, the areas include a mixture of whites and ethnic minorities. Other, more detailed research in Lewisham has shown that both across this borough with its comparatively high representation of minority groups and also within its relatively downmarket districts (specifically including multi-ethnic housing areas) whites have higher rates of drug misuse, on a last-year basis, than Afro-Caribbeans (Leitner et al., 1993). Indeed, that contrast was especially marked for the downmarket districts of the borough. Following that brief introduction, the remainder of this chapter is devoted to discussing drugs consumption on the part of different ethnic groups, as revealed by the 1996 BCS. Of course, what is offered is no more than a brief introduction.

Ethnicity

Minority ethnic groups account for scarcely six per cent of the population of England and Wales. However, the more recent sweeps of the BCS have included booster samples of Asians and Afro-Caribbeans, so as to increase their numbers over and above the few hundred ethnic minority respondents always included in the BCS core sample. The primary purpose of adding this booster sample has been to explore patterns of victimisation on the part of different ethnic minorities, which tend to be bleaker than those experienced by whites (FitzGerald and Hales, 1996). But the enlarged sample also makes it possible to explore drug misuse on the part of different ethnic groups.

Numbers and participation rates, ethnic booster

Over 2,000 extra people aged 16–59 were interviewed for the ethnic booster, providing a total contact sample of 13,488 (core sample equivalent, 11,244). As in the 1994 BCS, willingness to participate in the drugs self-report component was slightly lower for the enlarged sample, at 96 per cent as opposed to 97 per cent for the core sample alone. Different ethnic groups had varying participation rates: whites, 98 per cent; Afro-Caribbeans, 94 per cent; Indians, 87 per cent; Pakistanis/Bangladeshis, 78 per cent; and a small residual group of 'others', 85 per cent. (Further details on participation rates are provided in Table C.1, Appendix C.)

Table C.1 also shows that the proportion of ethnic minority respondents needing to be helped by the interviewer varied as between different groups: between seven per cent (Afro-Caribbeans) and 13 per cent (Pakistanis/Bangladeshis), as opposed to four per cent of whites. While it is conceivable that differences in the extent to which ethnic groups needed interviewer assistance could have had some effect on reported prevalence rates, it is also the case that those requiring help were less at risk of drug-taking, for instance because they tended to be relatively old. Comparison of Table C.1 with the equivalent table in the report on the 1994 BCS (Ramsay and Percy, 1996) shows that, across all groups, proportionately fewer respondents were given assistance in the 1996 BCS than in the 1994 BCS.

Altogether, there were 12,897 active participants in the enlarged self-report sample of the 1996 BCS. Apart from the whites (10,183), numbers for the different ethnic groups were relatively modest: 1,304 Afro-Caribbeans, 716 Indians, 415 Pakistanis/Bangladeshis, together with 279 others.

There is one other complication where ethnicity is concerned: differential recourse to the 'Don't Want to Answer' (DWA) option. In general, this occurred only to a modest extent, with the more common drugs, while its availability can perhaps be seen as safeguarding respondents' honesty. Thus, with cannabis, on the part of the 16–29 age group, two per cent of whites (and Indians and Pakistanis/Bangladeshis), as compared with four per cent of Afro-Caribbeans, chose the DWA option, which curtailed any further questioning about that particular drug. This does not matter greatly, given that around one in five of both whites and Afro-Caribbeans reported lifetime consumption of cannabis. Where it assumes greater importance is with drugs carrying the greatest stigma, notably heroin and crack cocaine. For some such drugs, the level of DWA responses on the part of certain groups came close to matching, or even exceeded, self-reported use. Given that DWA answers could signify conscious under-reporting, their effect needs to be remembered. Details, by drug and by ethnic group, are provided in Appendix C (Tables C.3 and C.4). Despite the DWA dimension, our general picture of levels of drug taking, on the part of different ethnic groups, is still reasonably reliable, at least where consumption on an ever/lifetime footing is concerned; particularly with 'any drug' or those less heavily stigmatised.

Ethnicity: results of the 1996 BCS drugs component

Ever/lifetime consumption of prohibited drugs necessarily constitutes the main focus. Our analysis takes its cue from two tables in this chapter. These tables illustrate patterns of drug taking by different ethnic groups, first the full age range (16-59) and then the more at-risk younger group (16–29).

Table 4.4, detailing ever/lifetime consumption by different ethnic groups (aged 16–59), is concerned with any drug, together with the two most widely consumed ones (cannabis, amphetamine), coupled with two others (heroin, crack cocaine) which cause especial concern. So far as any drug is concerned, whites have higher prevalence levels than Afro-Caribbeans, who in turn have higher levels than Indians or Pakistanis/Bangladeshis. A similar pattern applies with cannabis and amphetamine. Reported use of heroin and crack is universally at a very low level, with broadly comparable figures for all groups (almost non-existent in the case of those of Indian origin).

Table 4.4 Ethnic groups and drug taking: percentage of respondents aged 16–59 indicating they had ever taken certain drugs

	White	Afro-Caribbean	Indian	Pakistani/Bangladeshi
Cannabis	23	18	10	8
Amphetamine	9	6	2	2
Heroin	1	1	*	1
Crack	1	1	*	1
Any drug	30	23	14	12
N (unweighted)	10,183	1,304	716	415

Note: Source: 1996 BCS (core and booster samples combined, weighted data). The small and heterogeneous 'other' group has not been presented here or in other tables in this chapter, but relevant details are given in Appendix C (Table C.2). Figures relating to heroin and crack in particular need to be handled with care, since they are based on small numbers, especially in the case of ethnic minorities, and the reporting of their use may be affected by 'Don't Want to Answer' (DWA) responses (detailed in Appendix C, Table C.3).

This picture of drug misuse being – at least in general, and for the commoner drugs - more widespread on the part of whites than any other ethnic group, is confirmed and amplified when one turns instead to the 16–29 age range (Table 4.5). The gap between Afro-Caribbeans and whites, in terms of any drug taking ever, widens from a ratio of 1 to 1.3 for the full 16–59 age range (the 23/30% contrast shown in Table 4.4) to a ratio of 1 to 1.5 (the 31/46% contrast shown in Table 4.5). Where heroin and crack are concerned, Table 4.5 resembles Table 4.4 in showing similarly low prevalence rates for whites and Afro-Caribbeans; Pakistani/Bangladeshi consumption of heroin and crack by the 16–29 age group falls below the 0.5 per cent threshold.

Table 4.5 Ethnic groups and drug taking: percentage of respondents aged 16–29 indicating they had ever taken certain drugs

	White	Afro-Caribbean	Indian	Pakistani/Bangladeshi
Cannabis	38	26	18	11
Amphetamine	17	7	4	2
Heroin	1	1	0	*
Crack	1	1	*	*
Any drug	46	31	22	16
N (unweighted)	2,764	437	254	221

Note: Source: 1996 BCS (core and booster samples combined, weighted data). Figures relating to heroin and crack in particular need to be handled with care, since they are based on small numbers, especially in the case of ethnic minorities, and the reporting of their use may be affected by 'Don't Want to Answer' (DWA) responses (shown in Appendix C, Table C.3).

The final conclusion from Tables 4.4 and 4.5 is that, irrespective of age group, drug misuse is in general significantly more widespread on the part of whites than other ethnic groups. Only with comparatively little-used drugs such as heroin and crack are the prevalence levels similar for different ethnic groups. While, as the notes to the tables point out, the heroin/crack figures were affected by 'Don't Want to Answer' responses, these do not overturn the basic point that heroin and crack are only consumed by a tiny proportion of the population, with that small group including some members of minority groups as well as whites.

Ethnic groups and drug consumption: any changes?

The question of changing levels of drug misuse on the part of different ethnic groups, as between the 1994 and 1996 BCS, is not straightforward. So far, we have only considered drug taking on an ever/lifetime footing. The figures discussed above could be compared with those previously presented in the 1994 BCS drugs report (Ramsay and Percy, 1996). However, lifetime prevalence does not necessarily reflect recent usage. As it happens, consumption of drugs on an ever/lifetime footing, on the part of the different ethnic groups, did not change greatly as between the two different sweeps of the BCS: certainly not sufficiently to draw any clear conclusion. The only real exception to this general point was that, for Pakistanis/Bangldeshis, higher-than average figures for heroin prevalence in 1994 gave way to more or less average ones in 1996 but, in both years, total numbers of Pakistanis/Bangladeshis were modest, so that such fluctuations, for a little-used drug, are unsurprising.

Last-year consumption of drugs is a more appropriate point of comparison between the 1994 and 1996 BCS. There is however a difficulty, in that respondents' answers to questions about lifetime drug taking constrained the reporting of last-year prevalence – and, importantly, DWA opt-outs were not spread evenly across all groups. It was for precisely this reason that the report on the 1994 BCS drugs component stopped short of discussing last-year drug misuse by minorities. This was probably erring on the side of caution. While it would indeed be unwise to focus on last-year consumption by different ethnic groups of those little-used drugs where DWA opting out was relatively sizeable, in relation to reported prevalence levels, it is still feasible to assess last-year consumption of any drug or of cannabis, where DWA responses were not particularly pertinent. Indeed, while DWA opting out had some effect on the reporting of drug misuse on an ever/lifetime footing (especially with heavily stigmatised drugs), it was generally less in evidence with responses to questions concerning the last year.

What happened with last-year consumption of cannabis, the drug most readily and appropriately assessed on this footing, for the 1994 and 1996 BCS? A table in Appendix C (Table C.4), for the 16–29 and 16–59 age groups, shows that consumption of cannabis only increased slightly if at all on the part of both whites and minority groups, for both the full age range and the more at-risk younger group. That table also charts the extent of DWA opting out for each group, in relation to ever/lifetime and last-year questions on cannabis; it shows that DWA opting out was not particularly extensive, particularly in relation to the question about taking cannabis in the last year. Even more importantly, from the point of making comparisons between the two sweeps of the BCS, the table also shows that the extent to which respondents in the different ethnic groups selected DWA scarcely varied between 1994 and 1996.

Remembering that last point, we can now consider a table concerned with consumption of any drug by the four main ethnic groups in the 1994 and 1996 BCS, on the part of the 16–29 and 16–59 age groups. Obviously patterns of responses for cannabis, by far the most widely consumed drug, play a considerable part in determining these findings.

Table 4.6 Percentages of respondents in four main ethnic groups in the 1994 and 1996 BCS who indicated taking any drug in the last year, by age group

	White	Afro-Caribbean	Indian	Pakistani/Bangladeshi
16–29 age group				
1994 BCS	24	18	7	8
1996 BCS	25	19	10	10
16–59 age group				
1994 BCS	10	12	4	5
1996 BCS	10	10	5	6

Note: Source: 1994 and 1996 BCS (core and booster samples combined, weighted data). Unweighted numbers for different ethnic groups in the 1996 BCS are given in notes to previous tables in this chapter; for the 1994 BCS, when equivalent figures were slightly lower, they were as follows, starting with the full 16–59 age group: whites, 9,024; Afro-Caribbeans, 919; Indians, 554; Pakistanis/Bangladeshis, 406. For the 16–29 age group in the 1994 BCS, they were: whites, 2,550; Afro-Caribbeans, 329; Indians, 184; Pakistanis/Bangladeshis, 217. None of the changes shown in this table are significant, in terms of the criteria used elsewhere in this report.

This table confirms the lack of any significant change in last-year consumption of drugs on the part of different ethnic groups, from one sweep of the BCS to the next. Given the relatively small numbers of ethnic minority groups included even in the combined core/booster sample, some modest fluctuation is to be expected: it is not even consistently in the same direction, if both age groups are considered.

Having previously noted – in the last chapter – that there was no significant change in levels of misuse on the part of the main sample as between the 1994 and 1996 BCS, we can now conclude, albeit more tentatively, that the same holds true for the various ethnic groups.

5 Discussion

Measuring changes in drug misuse: different approaches

For many years, in the absence of any regular household survey, the prevalence of drug misuse in this country was apt to be measured through the Addicts Index. This annual statistical series, *Drug Addicts Notified to the Home Office* actually recorded the number of people assessed by doctors as addicts of heroin or cocaine (or various heroin-related drugs including methadone). In the late 1980s and early 1990s, annual increases in the number of registered addicts were consistently of the order of 20 per cent to 30 per cent or even higher still. This impression of rapidly escalating drug misuse is however potentially misleading. Arguably the increase reflects the expansion of treatment services – especially for those dependent on heroin – and not simply worsening drug misuse.

Certainly the BCS tells a very different story. We have already seen how, when comparing findings from the 1994 and 1996 BCS, the general picture is one of relatively stable drugs prevalence among the population at large. According to Addicts Index data for England and Wales in 1993 and 1995 (most nearly corresponding in time to the two last-year recall periods of the 1994/6 BCS), there was an increase of 31 per cent (Home Office, 1996). It is worth bearing in mind that, even in 1995, the total number of registered addicts in England and Wales, new and renotified, was less than 34,000.

Each set of figures has its own purpose. The Addicts Index – which has recently been closed – was a measure of the number of, mainly, heroin addicts in treatment, at the hands of GPs, hospitals and other treatment centres. Its role in counting those presenting for treatment has been replaced by a complementary and indeed substantially overlapping series, established fairly recently by the Department of Health, on the basis of information from Regional Drug Misuse Databases. This newer series enumerates those presenting for treatment of problems associated with a far wider range of drugs than in the Addicts Index, although heroin still features as the main drug of misuse.

Obviously there is some relationship between drug dependence and numbers of people treated for that dependence, both regionally and over time, but it may well be affected by the availability and popularity of service provision. One important reason why heroin has always featured far more prominently than cocaine in the Addicts Index (and in the Regional Drug Misuse Databases) is probably that drug treatment services have customarily been geared to meeting the needs of those dependent on heroin, who can be prescribed methadone by way of a substitute, while there is no such replacement for cocaine/crack. Yet from surveys such as the BCS it is apparent that the overall level of misuse of heroin is much the same as for crack cocaine.

While representative self-report surveys such as the BCS remain the best possible means of charting the extent of drug misuse on the part of the general population, they have certain limitations. As household surveys, they necessarily do not cover the tiny proportion of the total population that is homeless or those living in institutions, including prisons and residential educational establishments. In so far as people not living in settings routinely accessed by survey companies may have above-average levels of drug misuse, that is a drawback. It is one that can of course be addressed, at least in part, by specialist surveys focusing on those in schools, universities and other institutions, together with the homeless. It is also the case that household surveys, like other forms of self-reporting, may in various ways fall short in their coverage of drugs carrying the greatest social stigma, such as heroin and crack cocaine (as discussed in Chapter 2). However, even when such drawbacks have been taken into account, self-report surveys representative of the general population are uniquely powerful in revealing the extent and nature of drug misuse throughout the country. They chart drug taking in all its variety, rather than the provision of treatment for drug misuse. With survey limitations remaining broadly constant over time and place, this enables comparisons to be made between different regions and, when the same self-report procedures are repeated, in different years.

In the United States, the National Household Survey on Drug Abuse has been that country's main barometer of drug trends for over 20 years (Harrison, 1995); yet it is only in the last five years that equivalent surveys have developed in this country. As well as the BCS, there is the National Drugs Campaign Survey (NDCS) carried out by the Department of Health in collaboration with the Health Education Authority (HEA/BMRB, 1996; HEA/BMRB, 1997). The NDCS covers the 11–35 age range in England, initially using quota sampling (in 1995), and then a mixture of quota and – more authoritative – representative sampling (in 1996). Comparisons between the NDCS and the BCS are not entirely straightforward, but the results of the two surveys would seem mainly to be reasonably in line with each other, judging by NDCS results already published, those for 1995. The development of drugs surveys in this country is discussed elsewhere in greater detail (Ramsay and Percy, 1997).

Without regular and consistent drugs surveys in this country until almost the mid 1990s, we will never have a clear sense of what happened before then. Was drug consumption something that increased gradually and consistently between, say, the 1960s and the 1990s? Or was there slower and less regular growth, culminating in a surge of drug misuse in the late 1980s and very early 1990s? We can usefully rephrase those questions with another pair, also ultimately unanswerable: how far is drug misuse more extensive now than in the past and how far have we simply become more adept at assessing it? Efforts have occasionally been made to wrestle with some of these issues, on the basis of early attempts to survey self-reported drug misuse (Leitner et al., 1993; Mott and Mirrlees-Black, 1995), but considerable uncertainty remains.

The self-report sequence of questions developed for the BCS, with a paper questionnaire in 1992, subsequently adapted for respondents to tackle by means of laptop computers in 1994, has provided a format for various other drugs self-report exercises: the 1993 and 1996 Scottish Crime Surveys (paper versions), the 1994-5 Northern Ireland Crime Survey (laptop computer version), and - in England - the 1995 and 1996 National Drugs Campaign Survey (laptop versions). While those surveys have not all been published in full as yet, the fact that similar sequences of questions have been used should facilitate comparisons; although the mixture of paper questionnaires for some surveys and laptop sessions in others remains something of a complication (as do any variations in sampling procedures). Given that survey companies are increasingly turning to laptop computers both for their staff to use in carrying out interviews (computer-assisted personal interviewing or CAPI) and for any self-reporting by respondents (computer-assisted self-completion interviewing or CASI), this final anomaly may eventually disappear. Over the next few years, our already much enhanced understanding of patterns of drug misuse throughout the United Kingdom should improve still further.

Understanding the results of self-report surveys

The picture from national self-report surveys is of considerable one-off or experimental use of prohibited drugs by young people, together with an element of intermittent and more regular drug taking, as measured, approximately, by last-year and last-month perspectives.

However, self-report drugs surveys are sometimes misused to paint a picture of rampant drug misuse among young people. For instance, after Noel Gallagher's claim that "taking drugs is like having a cup of tea in the morning", a *New Musical Express* article (15 February 1997) asserted, on the basis of "1994 Home Office figures [showing that] 43 per cent of 16- to 29- year-olds have used illegal drugs", that this seriously damaged the credibility of the prevailing drugs policy. A similar argument, advanced by certain academics on the basis of findings from one particular self-report drugs survey carried out with young people in Liverpool and Manchester, is that drug taking is becoming 'normalised', as acceptable behaviour on the part of young people (Parker and Measham, 1994; Parker et al., 1995).

Quite clearly, in the mid 1990s, a substantial minority of young people – close to half – have at least experimented with prohibited drugs. But then young people have always been apt, on occasion, to run risks, flout authority or commit criminal offences. A large-scale sudy of self-reported offending (Graham and Bowling, 1995), covering both drug taking and crime in general, by young people aged 14–25, has shown that rather fewer have tried drugs (36%) than have committed a non-drugs criminal offence (43%). Indeed, it is a fact that, by the time they are in their mid-thirties, one in three of all young men will have been convicted of a criminal offence – excluding both drugs and driving offences – while many others will have committed offences of equal seriousness without being caught and convicted (Barclay et al., 1993).

In-depth studies of young people and their attitudes to drugs have shown that even in those circles where drug taking is comparatively widespread, both mutual and self-imposed limitations on drug-taking are important. For instance, a study of young people in Newham (Shiner and Newburn, 1996) noted that "non-users were by no means universally encouraged to use drugs by users. Some noted that their drug-using friends respected their decision not to use and others said that their drug-using friends had actively discouraged them from using drugs." That study concluded:

The breadth of opinion expressed by respondents, and in particular the prevalence of negative opinions, challenged the idea contained in the normalisation thesis (whether explicit or not) that drug use is generally considered to be acceptable by young people.

It seems that young people growing up in this country are very likely, at some point, to come across prohibited drugs; a majority may well have been in situations where drugs have been on offer, perhaps from friends (Parker and Measham, 1994; Balding, 1995; Wright and Pearl, 1995). In this sense, drugs are present in the lives of many if not most young people, as something they are likely to encounter but not necessarily accept.

However, less than half of all young people actually do try drugs (45% of 16–29s, according to the 1996 BCS). As to any more frequent consumption of drugs, the involvement of young people falls markedly. On a last-year footing, only 24 per cent have taken prohibited drugs. Where the last month is concerned, no more than 15 per cent have done so. Arguably this relatively small group, for most of whom drug taking is regular, should be of equal or greater concern than the "one in two" young people (or thereabouts) who at some point(s) in their lives have taken drugs.

An interesting qualitative study of young people with considerable experience of prohibited 'dance' drugs such as ecstasy and amphetamine concludes:

> In the broader context of the young people's lifestyles, drugs were not viewed as a priority. Most stated that being with family and friends was the main priority in their lives.

That study also confirms the point made by Shiner and Newburn, that peer pressure was not seen as an important factor, except in relation to a legal drug, tobacco. And it points to a range of self-imposed controls by these "recreational drug users", such as not taking drugs too often, not injecting, staying well clear of heroin and being cautious in relation to cocaine (Power et al., 1996).

Surveys such as the BCS point, ultimately, to a series of paradoxes. On the one hand, drug misuse can be found right across society, although especially damaging drug misuse is more likely in impoverished settings. So far as most young people are concerned, it is not a regular feature of their lives, even though a majority can expect to come across drug taking or be offered prohibited drugs by friends and acquaintances. There can indeed be peer pressure: but this may be more relevant with legal drugs than prohibited ones. And, finally, while consumption of prohibited drugs is not currently escalating across the country as a whole, it does seem to be increasing in certain regions.

A key performance indicator (KPI) for the drugs strategy

The 1995 White Paper, *Tackling Drugs Together: a Strategy for England 1995-1998*, identifies drug misuse by under-25s as a key performance indicator. To that end, the BCS provides figures which help to show what was happening as an enhanced drugs strategy was starting to come into effect. Table 5.1 shows ever/lifetime, last year and last month prevalence data for any drug, for the 16–24 age group, from the 1994 and 1996 BCS.

Table 5.1 Percentages of respondents aged 16–24 in the 1994 and 1996 BCS who used any drug ever or in the last year or month

	Ever/ lifetime	Last year	Last month
1994 BCS	45	29	17
1996 BCS	48	29	18

Note: The last year, in the case of the 1994 BCS, was a twelve month period between early 1993 and early 1994; the last-year period for the 1996 BCS was between equivalent points early in 1995 and 1996. The White Paper on drugs was published in May 1995, a little way into the second of the two last-year periods. Source: 1994 and 1996 BCS (core samples, weighted data).

This table reiterates the general point made throughout this report, that drug misuse has been relatively stable as between the two sweeps of the BCS. The last-year perspective, probably the best point of comparison, suggests a complete absence of change, with 29 per cent of the 16–24 age group reporting misuse of any drug in both the 1994 and 1996 BCS.

It would be unwise to claim that this relatively stable level of drug misuse on the part of the general population is a direct outcome of the recently established drugs strategy, given that the two developments were more or less contemporaneous. The next sweep of the BCS, in 1998, should provide clearer testimony as to what is happening to prevalence levels, in terms of national, regional and other trends.

Appendix A: Response rate and other survey details for the core sample

The BCS is a well established survey, and further details are available from a variety of sources. The principal results of the 1996 sweep – focusing mainly on victimisation from crime – were first published as a Home Office Statistical Bulletin (Mirrlees-Black et al., 1996). There is also a technical report, produced by SCPR, which was responsible for the fieldwork and data processing (Hales and Stratford, 1997). This appendix simply gives a succinct overview of the sampling process for the core sample, leaving consideration of the ethnic booster to Appendix C. (The ethnic booster sample was only drawn on for the part of Chapter 4 concerned with different ethnic groups.)

Those who are interested in further information on the technical side – over and above that presented here – should turn to Hales and Stratford (1997), for instance, for details on sampling errors and design effects. In line with normal practice with the BCS, a data tape (with supporting material) will be made accessible to the research community, through the ESRC Data Archive at the University of Essex. The 1994 BCS has already been made available through the Data Archive.

Survey process and response rate for the 1996 BCS

As mentioned in Chapter 1, the BCS is a nationally representative survey, covering the population of England and Wales aged 16 and above. Altogether, 16,348 people were successfully interviewed, typically for over an hour's duration, most of this time being devoted to questioning about possible victimisation from crime. Interviewing took place in the first few months of 1996, being 99 per cent complete at the end of April, but with a few final interviews as late as June.

Interviewing was organised and carried out by staff of SCPR. The sample frame was the small-user postcode address file (PAF). Actual sampling units comprised 800 postcode sectors, with systematic selection on a random basis from a stratified list of postcode sectors. The preliminary stratification exercise involved: inner-city and other areas; standard regions; population density; and social class of heads of household. Within households, final selection of individuals for interviewing was done randomly. The response rate was 83 per cent, the highest ever for the BCS, and a high one for any household survey of the general population. Coverage of the population of England and Wales in terms of age groups, gender and other key variables was generally satisfactory.

In line with normal practice, the data obtained from the survey process were later adjusted or 'weighted' to ensure that households in different areas (such as inner city or not) or at matching addresses, and also individuals in households of different sizes, all had equal chances of selection. The percentages presented in the main part of this report are all based on this weighted data.

Completing the drugs self-report component

There were actually two self-completion components in the 1996 BCS, covering not only illegal drugs but also domestic violence. These two components were only put to respondents in the 16–59 age bracket, excluding those who were aged 60 and over. Interviewers gave a brief introduction to the content and format of the self-completion element and then turned the computer round and handed it over to the respondent. Respondents followed instructions given to them on the screen.

Respondents were strongly encouraged to use the lap-top computers themselves; only in the last resort were they helped, with the interviewer keying in the answers. There was no pen and paper fallback.

Participation in the drugs self-report component: assisted and unassisted

The relevant contact sample for the drugs self-report component of the 1994 BCS numbered 11,244. There were 304 refusals, leaving 10,940 as the baseline.

Whether because of a change from one survey company to another, or simply on account of greater familiarity with computers on the part of survey companies and/or the public, proportionately fewer respondents tackling the drugs self-report needed to be helped by the interviewer in the 1996 BCS as compared with the 1994 sweep. The reduction was from nine per cent down to five per cent (unweighted numbers were 893 out of 9,646 participants in the 1994 BCS and 551 out of 10,940 participants in the 1996 BCS). This change applied relatively evenly with different age groups. Similarly, there was a consistent reduction among both males and females, with both rates falling from nine per cent down to five per cent.

As discussed in the same appendix for the 1994 BCS (Ramsay and Percy, 1996), those needing help were disproportionately 'stay-at-homes': a marker for relatively low levels of drug misuse. This continued to be the case in 1996. For instance, in 1996, 47 per cent of those helped by the interviewer reported that they did not go to a pub in the last month; for those not helped, the equivalent figure was 32 per cent. Age was an important factor, but not overwhelmingly so (assistance rates, 5% on average, were in the range of 2% to 7%, for 16-19 and 40-59 year olds respectively).

With a significant reduction in the number of interviewees requiring assistance, between the 1994 and 1996 BCS, it is probably unsurprising that, on the part of this small and increasingly unusual group, there was – across the full 16-59 age range – a slight reduction in the proportion reporting any drug misuse (ever), which dropped from 18.5 per cent to 15.2 per cent. Among those not helped, corresponding figures increased marginally, from 29.4 to 29.6 per cent. But these are all non-significant changes. And it is interesting that there was also an increase in the proportion of those helped who said that they never went out: from 5.7 per cent to 10.2 per cent.

Ultimately, so few people were helped, especially in the 1996 BCS, that any effect on overall reporting rates could only have been marginal. Those who were helped did not report substantially lower rates of drug misuse than those who were not helped; such as it was, the contrast reflected, at least in part, the different characteristics of these two sets of people.

Calculating the drugs component participation rate

Given that both those who self-completed the drugs component without any assistance from the interviewer and the minority of individuals who were helped can be deemed to have participated, it may be helpful to provide a table summarising participation rates for the 1994 and 1996 BCS. The proportion participating fell slightly, from 97.5 per cent to 97.3 per cent.

Table A.1 Participation rates for 1994 and 1996 BCS (16–59 age group)

	1994 No.	1994 %	1996 No.	1996 %
Refused to participate	241	2.4	304	2.7
Don't know	2	0.0	0	0
Respondent self-completion	8,753	88.5	10,389	92.4
Assisted self-completion	893	9.0	551	4.9
Total (contact sample)	9,889	100	11,244	100
Of which: **all participants**, respondent and assisted self-completion	9,646	97.5	10,940	97.3

As discussed elsewhere, in the main part of this report, participation – whether unassisted or not – in the drugs self-report component does not guarantee total honesty on the part of the respondents. It is likely that, as with surveys of alcohol consumption, smoking and eating chocolate, there is some under-reporting. However, respondents were also allowed a 'don't want to answer' (DWA) option for each substance. In general, at least within the main sample, very little use was made of this opt-out (down to 0.2% for some substances). A rather higher rate of use of DWA occurred within the ethnic booster sample and, accordingly, there is further discussion of the DWA phenomenon in Chapter 4 and Appendix C.

One final point worth noting, given the emphasis placed on the 16–29 age group in this report, is that there were altogether 3,026 (unweighted), accounting for 28 per cent of all 10,940 participants in the 1996 BCS drugs self-report component.

Appendix B: Supplementary tables

Table B.1:Percentages of respondents who said they had heard of the drugs

	16-29 age group	30-59 age group	16-59 age group (i.e. all)
Cannabis	98	97	98
Amphetamines	94	92	93
LSD	97	97	97
Magic mushrooms	92	80	84
Ecstasy	98	98	98
Valium, temazepam	94	96	96
Cocaine	99	98	99
Crack	94	94	94
Methadone	64	74	71
Heroin	98	98	98
Poppers	73	63	66
Steroids	95	95	95
Semeron	5	3	4

Source: 1996 BCS (core sample, weighted data). Semeron is a bogus substance.

Table B.2: Percentages of males and females who indicated that they had ever taken particular drugs, by age group

	16-19	20-24	25-29	30-34	35-39	40-44	45-59	All 16-59	All 16-29
Cannabis									
M	38	48	39	35	29	30	10	27	42
F	32	36	27	21	18	15	5	18	31
All	35	42	32	27	23	23	8	22	36
Amphetamines									
M	15	26	15	13	10	10	4	11	18
F	17	16	10	7	6	3	2	7	13
All	16	21	12	10	8	7	3	9	16
LSD									
M	12	21	9	8	5	8	2	7	13
F	8	9	5	2	2	2	*	3	7
All	10	14	7	5	4	5	1	5	10
Magic Mushrooms									
M	10	17	11	10	8	5	2	7	12
F	4	7	6	5	3	2	*	3	6
All	7	12	8	8	5	3	1	5	9
Smoke unknown									
M	9	8	5	5	4	5	1	4	7
F	10	6	5	3	2	1	1	3	6
All	9	7	5	4	3	3	1	4	7
Ecstasy									
M	9	19	6	5	1	1	1	5	11
F	8	8	5	2	1	*	*	2	7
All	9	13	5	3	1	1	1	3	9
Temazepam, etc.									
M	5	4	2	3	4	5	2	3	3
F	4	3	2	2	4	3	4	3	3
All	4	3	2	3	4	4	3	3	3
Glue, etc.									
M	5	9	7	3	1	1	*	3	7
F	5	5	3	1	*	0	*	1	4
All	5	7	5	2	1	1	*	2	5
Cocaine									
M	3	9	4	6	5	4	2	4	5
F	*	3	3	2	2	1	1	2	3
All	2	6	4	4	4	3	1	3	4
Pills									
M	4	4	1	1	2	2	1	2	3
F	1	3	1	1	1	1	*	1	2
All	3	4	1	1	1	1	1	1	2

Table B.2: contd.

	16–19	20–24	25–29	30–34	35–39	40–44	45–59	All 16–59	All 16–29
Crack									
M	2	3	1	*	2	1	1	1	2
F	0	1	*	1	*	*	*	*	1
All	1	2	1	*	1	*	*	1	1
Methadone									
M	1	0	*	1	1	1	*	*	*
F	*	1	*	*	0	*	*	*	*
All	1	*	*	*	*	*	*	*	*
Heroin									
M	2	1	1	2	1	1	1	1	1
F	0	1	*	*	0	*	*	*	*
All	1	1	*	1	*	1	*	1	1
Poppers									
M	14	26	16	12	5	5	1	9	18
F	11	10	7	4	2	1	*	4	9
All	13	17	11	8	3	3	1	6	14
Steroids									
M	1	3	2	2	1	1	1	1	2
F	0	1	1	1	*	1	1	1	1
All	1	2	1	2	1	1	1	1	1
Semeron									
M	0	0	*	*	0	0	*	*	*
F	0	0	0	*	0	0	0	*	0
All	0	0	*	*	0	0	*	*	*
Anything else									
M	1	2	1	1	1	2	*	1	1
F	2	2	1	*	*	*	*	1	1
All	1	2	1	1	*	1	*	1	1
Any drug									
M	48	57	48	42	36	38	15	34	50
F	42	43	35	28	24	20	11	24	39
All	45	49	41	34	30	28	13	29	45

* Less than 0.5%.

Source: 1996 BCS, weighted data. Semeron is a bogus substance

Table B.3: Percentages of males and females who indicated that they had taken particular drugs in the last year, by age group

	16–19	20–24	25–29	30–34	35–39	40–44	45–59	All 16-59	All 16-29
Cannabis									
M	29	29	19	11	6	6	2	11	25
F	25	20	11	5	4	2	1	7	17
All	27	24	15	8	5	4	1	9	21
Amphetamines									
M	11	17	5	3	1	*	*	4	11
F	12	6	3	1	1	*	*	2	6
All	12	11	4	2	1	*	*	3	8
LSD									
M	8	7	1	1	0	*	*	2	5
F	2	1	*	*	0	0	*	*	1
All	5	3	1	*	0	*	*	1	3
Magic Mushrooms									
M	3	5	1	*	*	*	*	1	3
F	1	*	*	1	0	0	*	*	1
All	2	2	1	*	*	*	*	1	2
Smoke unknown									
M	4	1	*	*	*	*	*	1	2
F	2	2	*	*	*	0	*	*	1
All	3	2	*	*	*	*	*	1	1
Ecstasy									
M	6	11	2	1	*	*	*	2	6
F	6	3	2	*	*	*	*	1	3
All	6	6	2	1	*	*	*	1	4
Temazepam, etc.									
M	2	1	*	1	1	1	*	*	1
F	2	*	*	*	*	*	*	*	1
All	2	*	*	1	*	*	*	*	1
Glue, etc.									
M	1	1	*	*	0	0	*	*	1
F	1	*	0	0	0	0	*	*	*
All	1	*	*	*	0	0	*	*	*
Cocaine									
M	1	3	1	1	*	*	*	1	2
F	*	1	2	*	*	0	*	*	1
All	1	2	1	1	*	*	*	1	1
Pills									
M	*	1	*	*	*	0	*	*	*
F	1	*	*	*	0	0	*	*	*
All	*	*	*	*	*	0	*	*	*

Table B.3: contd.

	16-19	20-24	25-29	30-34	35-39	40-44	45-59	All 16-59	All 16-29
Crack									
M	1	0	*	0	*	0	*	*	*
F	0	*	0	0	0	0	*	*	*
All	*	*	*	0	*	0	*	*	*
Methadone									
M	*	0	*	*	*	0	*	*	*
F	0	*	*	0	0	0	*	*	*
All	*	*	*	*	*	0	*	*	*
Heroin									
M	1	*	*	*	*	*	*	*	*
F	0	*	*	*	0	0	*	*	*
All	*	*	*	*	*	*	*	*	*
Poppers									
M	5	7	2	1	1	1	*	2	4
F	6	2	1	*	*	0	*	1	2
All	5	4	2	1	1	1	*	1	3
Steroids									
M	*	1	1	*	*	0	*	*	1
F	0	1	*	*	*	*	*	*	*
All	*	1	*	*	*	*	*	*	*
Semeron									
M	0	0	0	0	0	0	*	*	0
F	0	0	0	*	0	0	0	*	0
All	0	0	0	*	0	0	*	*	0
Anything else									
M	*	*	*	*	0	0	*	*	*
F	*	*	0	0	0	0	*	*	*
All	*	*	*	*	0	0	*	*	*
Any drug									
M	35	32	22	13	9	7	2	13	29
F	27	23	13	6	5	3	1	8	20
All	31	27	17	9	7	5	2	10	24

* Less than 0.5%

Source 1996 BCS, weighted data. Semeron is a bogus substance

Table B.4: Percentages of males and females who indicated that they had taken particular drugs in the last month, by age group

	16-19	20-24	25-29	30-34	35-39	40-44	45-59	All 16-59	All 16-29
Cannabis									
M	19	22	10	6	4	3	1	7	16
F	12	11	6	2	3	1	*	3	9
All	16	16	8	4	3	2	1	5	12
Amphetamines									
M	6	9	3	2	*	*	*	2	6
F	4	2	1	*	*	*	*	1	2
All	5	6	2	1	*	*	*	1	4
LSD									
M	2	1	*	*	0	*	*	*	1
F	1	*	*	0	0	0	*	*	*
All	1	1	*	*	0	*	*	*	1
Magic Mushrooms									
M	1	*	*	*	0	*	*	*	*
F	1	*	0	0	0	0	*	*	*
All	1	*	*	*	0	*	*	*	*
Smoke unknown									
M	2	*	*	*	0	0	*	*	1
F	1	1	*	*	0	0	*	*	1
All	1	*	*	*	0	0	*	*	1
Ecstasy									
M	3	5	1	*	*	0	*	1	3
F	2	1	1	*	*	0	*	*	1
All	2	3	1	*	*	0	*	1	2
Temazepam, etc.									
M	1	*	*	*	*	*	*	*	*
F	1	*	*	*	*	0	*	*	*
All	1	*	*	*	*	*	*	*	*
Glue, etc.									
M	*	*	0	*	0	0	*	*	*
F	0	*	0	0	0	0	*	*	*
All	*	*	0	*	0	0	*	*	*
Cocaine									
M	*	1	1	*	*	*	*	*	1
F	*	0	*	*	*	0	*	*	*
All	*	*	*	*	*	*	*	*	*
Pills									
M	0	*	*	*	*	0	*	*	*
F	*	*	0	*	0	0	*	*	*
All	*	*	*	*	*	0	*	*	*

Table B.4: cont.

	16-19	20-24	25-29	30-34	35-39	40-44	45-59	All 16-59	All 16-29
Crack									
M	1	0	*	0	0	0	*	*	*
F	0	0	0	0	0	0	*	*	0
All	*	0	*	0	0	0	*	*	*
Methadone									
M	0	0	0	0	*	0	*	*	0
F	0	*	*	0	0	0	*	*	*
All	0	*	*	0	*	0	*	*	*
Heroin									
M	0	0	0	*	*	0	*	*	0
F	0	*	*	*	0	0	*	*	*
All	0	*	*	*	*	0	*	*	*
Poppers									
M	2	2	1	1	1	1	*	1	1
F	3	*	*	*	0	0	*	*	1
All	2	1	*	*	*	*	*	*	1
Steroids									
M	0	0	*	*	*	0	*	*	*
F	0	*	*	*	*	*	*	*	*
All	0	*	*	*	*	*	*	*	*
Semeron									
M	0	0	0	0	0	0	0	0	0
F	0	0	0	*	0	0	0	*	0
All	0	0	0	*	0	0	0	*	0
Anything else									
M	*	*	*	*	0	0	*	*	*
F	*	0	0	0	0	0	*	*	*
All	*	*	*	*	0	0	*	*	*
Any drug									
M	23	24	13	7	5	4	1	8	19
F	15	12	7	3	3	2	1	4	10
All	19	18	10	5	4	3	1	6	15

* Less than 0.5%

Source: 1996 BCS, weighted data, Semeron is a bogus substance.

Table B.5: Percentages of respondents consuming different levels of alcohol who have used drugs ever or in the last year or month, by age group

	Never	Light drinker	Moderate drinker	Heavy drinker	Average
Ever/lifetime					
16–29	20	37	55	70	45
30–59	12	19	29	36	22
All	14	24	37	48	29
Last year					
16–29	9	17	30	48	24
30–59	2	3	5	10	4
All	4	7	12	23	10
Last month					
16–29	6	9	18	31	15
30–59	1	2	3	6	2
All	2	4	7	15	6

Source: 1996 BCS (weighted data). Heavy drinkers comprise those consuming 2+ units a day; moderate drinkers those on one or more units a day (but less than two); light drinkers are those on less than one unit a day. The proportion of respondents in each category was: heavy drinkers, 16%; moderate drinkers, 17%; light drinkers, 56%; non-drinkers, 11%. Those who did not know their alcohol consumption or refused to dislose it have been excluded.

Table B.6:Percentages of smoking/non-smoking respondents who used drugs ever or in the last year or month, by age group

	Smokers	Non-smokers	Average
Ever/lifetime			
16–29	66	33	45
30–59	31	19	22
All	42	23	29
Last year			
16–29	40	15	24
30–59	8	3	4
All	19	6	10
Last month			
16–29	26	8	15
30-59	5	1	2
All	12	3	6

Source: 1996 BCS (weighted data). Smokers comprised 32% of the sample, non-smokers 68%.

Table B.7 Percentages of respondents aged 16-24 in the 1994 and 1996 BCS who used any drug within the last year, by different years of age

	1994 BCS: drug use within last year	1996 BCS: drug use within last year
Age 16	29	34
Age 17	33	29
Age 18	33	29
Age 19	40	32
Age 20	26	28
Age 21	36	31
Age 22	23	32
Age 23	21	28
Age 24	20	18

Note: Sources: 1994 and 1996 BCS (weighted data). For the 16-24 age group as a whole, the total N was 1,445 in the 1994 BCS (average 161 per year group); 1,477 in the 1996 BCS (average 164 per year group).

Appendix C: Minority ethnic booster sample

Introduction

By way of supplement to the latter part of Chapter 4, this appendix provides additional information on the minority ethnic boost sample, in association with the core sample, and differentiating the various ethnic groups. Further information is provided in the technical report for the 1996 BCS (Hales and Stratford, 1997).

In 1996, the ethnic booster sample was selected in two ways:

- *Focused enumeration.* This involves interviewers screening households close to those already selected for the core sample, to ascertain the presence of those from ethnic minorities (Black or Asian). Focused enumeration was carried out in areas known to have ethnic minority reresentation, broadly in line with procedures used in the 1994 BCS, although in 1996 the number of households screened was reduced from three to two, to left and to right of core sample households. Normal procedures were followed to select ethnic minority household members for interview.

- *Sampling of areas known to have high representation of ethnic minorities.* To compensate for the reduced number of households screened through focused enumeration in 1996, additional addresses in areas with high representation of ethnic minorities were sampled, using normal random-selection procedures. Only household members frm ethnic minorities were eligible for interview.

Together, these two methods considerably enhanced the yield of ethnic booster sample addresses. The higher response rate achieved with both core and booster sample households also helped to bring this about.

Participation rate and associated details

Focusing on the enlarged sample with the ethnic boost, the first key point is that participation rates for the various non-white groups were lower than for whites (or for all those in the main sample alone). This emerges clearly from a preliminary table presenting the combined core/boost ethnic participation rates:

	White	Afro-Caribbean	Indian	Pakistani/Bangladeshi
1. Contact sample	10,379	1,383	837	552
2. Non-participants	196	79	121	137
3. Base, self-report	10,183	1,304	716	415
4. Participation rate (3/1)	98.1%	94.3%	85.5%	75.2%

Note: The "other" group has not been presented above, in line with practice in Chapter 4. This residual group is both small and varied. For reference, equivalent figures for this group were: (1) 379; (2) 62; (3) 317; (4) 83.6 per cent. For the combined core/boost sample as a whole, including the other group, the figures were: (1) 13,530; (2) 595; (3) 12,935; (4) 95.6 per cent. Source: 1996 BCS, unweighted data, core sample and boost.

In the combined sample, almost twice as many people refused to take part as in the core sample, although the combined sample is barely 20 per cent bigger than the main sample. In the 1996 BCS there were only straightforward acceptances/refusals, rather than any "don't knows"/"don't want to answer", in response to the question on partication. Language problems, mentioned by over half the ethnic boost respondents who declined to take part in the self-report, were by far the most commonly expressed reason for refusal to participate.

As with the 1994 BCS, the sample is just sufficiently large to make it possible to differentiate within the Asian group between Indians on the one hand and Pakistanis and Bangladeshis on the other. This is helpful, given that the pattern of responses to the question on participation in the drugs self-report exercise differed between these two sets of people. There was also some further variation in their respective patterns of drug use (as discussed in Chapter 4).

White respondents were less likely to opt out from the drugs self-report exercise than were non-whites. Whites were also less likely to need to be helped by the interviewer. Focusing on responses to the question about willingness to participate, one finds the following variation, in percentage terms:

Table C.1 Ethnic groups and their response to the drugs self-report, showing percentages accepting or refusing to participate

	White	Afro-Caribbean	Indian	Pakistani/Bangladeshi
Accepted (not helped)	94.1	86.7	79.0	65.4
Accepted (needed help)	4.2	7.2	7.5	12.6
TOTAL THAT ACCEPTED	98.3	93.9	86.5	78.0
Refused to participate	1.7	6.1	13.4	22.0
N per group (total contacted)	10,379	1,383	837	552

Note: Source is 1996 BCS core sample and ethnic boost (weighted data: although the Ns in the bottom row are unweighted). The "other" group of respondents, 379 of whom were originally contacted (unweighted N), has not been shown above. As a small and heterogeneous group, there is limited value in detailing their results – which are not given in Chapter 4 or elsewhere in this appendix (nor are they usually provided in BCS reports). However, in terms of this table, 78.9 per cent of the other group accepted without being helped, while seven per cent accepted but needed help: leaving the total that accepted as 85.9 per cent, with 14.1 per cent refusing to participate.

This table makes it quite clear that acceptance varied by ethnic group, with the highest rate for whites (98.3% accepting, or 1.7% refusing) and then successively lower rates for Afro-Caribbeans, Indians and Pakistanis/Bangladeshis.

The remainder of this appendix is devoted to tables showing, respectively, percentages of respondents in different ethnic groups who indicated that they had ever taken particular drugs (Table C.2); percentages of respondents in different ethnic groups who gave 'Don't want to answer' (DWA) responses on an ever/lifetime footing (Table C.3); and finally, percentages of 1994 and 1996 respondents admitting consumption of cannabis in the last year or else selecting DWA responses for cannabis, both ever/lifetime and for the last year (Table C.4).

Table C.2 Percentages of respondents in different ethnic groups who indicated that they had ever taken particular drugs, with contrasting age groups

	White	Afro-Caribbean	Indian	Pakistani/Bangladeshi
Cannabis				
16–29	38	26	18	11
30–59	17	13	5	5
All, 16–59	23	18	10	8
Amphetamines				
16–29	17	7	4	2
30–59	6	4	1	1
All, 16–59	9	6	2	2
LSD				
16–29	10	5	3	1
30–59	3	1	1	*
All, 16–59	5	2	2	1
Magic mushrooms				
16–29	9	4	1	3
30–59	3	1	1	*
All, 16–59	5	2	1	2
Smoke unknown				
16–29	7	5	4	1
30–59	2	2	2	1
All, 16–59	4	3	3	1
Ecstasy				
16–29	9	7	2	1
30–59	1	1	1	1
All, 16–59	3	3	1	1
Temazepam, etc.				
16–29	3	2	*	1
30–59	3	2	1	1
All, 16–59	3	2	1	1

	White	Afro-Caribbean	Indian	Pakistani/Bangladeshi
Glue, etc.				
16–29	6	2	*	3
30–59	1	1	*	*
All, 16–59	2	1	*	2
Cocaine				
16–29	3	2	2	2
30–59	2	1	1	1
All, 16–59	3	2	1	2
Pills unknown				
16–29	2	2	2	2
30–59	1	1	1	1
All, 16–59	1	1	1	1
Crack				
16–29	1	1	*	*
30–59	*	*	*	1
All, 16–59	1	1	*	1
Methadone				
16–29	*	*	0	*
30–59	*	1	*	*
All, 16–59	*	*	*	*
Heroin				
16–29	1	1	0	*
30–59	1	1	*	1
All, 16–59	1	1	*	1
Poppers				
16–29	14	6	2	3
30–59	3	1	1	1
All, 16–59	6	3	1	2
Steroids				
16–29	2	*	*	1
30–59	1	1	1	1
All, 16–59	1	1	1	1

	White	Afro-Caribbean	Indian	Pakistani/Bangladeshi
Semeron				
16–29	0	*	0	0
30–59	0	0	0	*
All, 16–59	0	0	0	*
Anything else				
16–29	1	*	2	1
30–59	1	*	*	0
All, 16–59	1	*	1	*
Any drug				
16–29	46	31	22	16
30–59	23	19	9	6
All, 16–59	30	23	14	12

Note: Source: 1996 BCS core sample and ethnic boost (weighted data). Figures for the 'other' group are not shown above. Unweighted numbers were as follows: whites, 10,183; Afro-Caribbeans, 1,304; Indians, 716; Pakistanis/Bangladeshis, 415; others, 317 (N = 12,935). In line with general practice in this report, figures under 0.5 are shown as * and those where there were no respondents as 0. Semeron is a bogus drug.

Table C.3 Percentages of respondents in different ethnic groups who gave different 'Don't want to answer' (DWA) responses, with contrasting age groups

	White	Afro-Caribbean	Indian	Pakistani/Bangladeshi
Cannabis				
16–29	2	4	2	2
30–59	0.5	1	0.7	0.2
All, 16–59	0.8	2	1	1
Amphetamines				
16–29	2	2	0.7	0.8
30–59	0.4	0.5	0.5	0
All, 16–59	0.7	0.9	0.6	0.5
LSD				
16–29	0.9	1	0.7	0.8
30–59	0.3	0.4	0.3	0
All, 16–59	0.5	0.8	0.5	0.5
Magic mushrooms				
16–29	0.7	1	2	0.4
30–59	0.2	0.4	0.3	0
All, 16–59	0.4	0.7	1	0.2
Smoke unknown				
16–29	0.6	0.9	0.7	0.4
30–59	0.3	0.5	0.5	0
All, 16–59	0.4	0.6	0.6	0.2
Ecstasy				
16–29	1	2	0.7	0.4
30–59	0.2	0.4	0.3	0
All, 16–59	0.5	1	0.5	0.2
Temazepam etc.				
16–29	0.3	0.6	0.3	0.4
30–59	0.2	0.2	0.3	0
All, 16–59	0.2	0.4	0.3	0.2

Table C.3: Contd.

	White	Afro-Caribbean	Indian	Pakistani/Bangladeshi
Glue, etc.				
16–29	0.8	2	2	0.6
30–59	0.2	0.3	0.7	0
All, 16–59	0.3	0.8	1	0.3
Cocaine				
16–29	0.9	2	0.7	0.4
30–59	0.2	0.5	0.8	0
All, 16–59	0.4	1	0.8	0.2
Pills unknown				
16–29	0.7	2	2	2
30–59	0.2	0.3	0.7	0
All, 16–59	0.4	0.7	1	1
Crack				
16–29	0.4	2	0.7	0.4
30–59	0.2	0.4	0.4	0
All, 16–59	0.2	1	0.6	0.2
Methadone				
16–29	0.3	1	1	0.4
30–59	0.2	0.4	0.3	0
All, 16–59	0.2	0.8	0.6	0.2
Heroin				
16–29	0.3	2	0.7	0.4
30–59	0.2	0.4	0.3	0.4
All, 16–59	0.2	0.9	0.5	0.4
Poppers				
16–29	0.8	0.6	1	0.4
30–59	0.2	0.4	0.4	0
All, 16–59	0.4	0.5	0.7	0.2
Steroids				
16–29	0.3	1	0.7	0.6
30–59	0.2	0.4	0.3	0
All, 16–59	0.2	0.5	0.5	0.3

Table C.3: Contd.

	White	Afro-Caribbean	Indian	Pakistani/Bangladeshi
Semeron				
16–29	0	0.5	0.8	0
30–59	0	0.1	0	0
All, 16–59	0	0.3	0.4	0
Anything else				
16–29	0.4	1	1	0.4
30–59	0.2	0.2	0.6	0
All, 16–59	0.3	0.5	0.8	0.2

Note: Source: 1996 BCS core sample and ethnic boost (weighted data). Figures for the 'other' group are not shown. N = 12,618, without the other group; 12,935, including them. In this table, numbers below 1 are given to the nearest decimal point, to avoid a table characterised by asterisks (used elsewhere for numbers less than 0.5). There is no 'any drug' component to this table, which illustrates the – generally low – level of DWA responses for individual types of drug. Semeron is a bogus drug.

Table C.4 Percentages of respondents in different ethnic groups for 1994 and 1996 BCS who indicated that they had taken cannabis in last year, or gave DWA responses for cannabis ever or last year

	16–29 age group		16–59 age group	
	1994	1996	1994	1996
White				
Use cannabis, year	21	22	8	9
DWA cannabis, ever	2	2	0.8	0.8
DWA cannabis, year	0.4	0.6	0.2	0.2
Afro-Caribbean				
Use cannabis, year	16	17	10	9
DWA cannabis, ever	4	4	2	2
DWA cannabis, year	0	0	0	0
Indian				
Use cannabis, year	5	8	3	4
DWA cannabis, ever	2	2	1	1
DWA cannabis, year	2	2	0.6	1
Pakistani/Bangladeshi				
Use cannabis, year	6	8	4	5
DWA cannabis, ever	0.5	2	0.3	1
DWA cannabis, year	0	0	0	0

Sources: 1994 and 1996 BCS core sample and ethnic boost (weighted data). In this table, all numbers below one are given to the nearest decimal point. If one were to assume that DWA (Don't Want to Answer) responses were given by those reluctant to admit to consuming a drug - in this case, cannabis, on a last-year footing - then there would be a case for adding the DWA percentages (ever and last year) to the percentages of those openly admitting to consumption of cannabis. It is however impossible to be sure of this assumption, on any general basis.

Appendix D: Injecting of drugs

The only substantive change to the BCS drugs self-completion section since 1994 has been the introduction of a question on the injecting of drugs. Respondents who had admitted using any drug in the last year, excluding cannabis, smoke unknown and Semeron, were asked the following question:

> *[This is the last question in the drugs section of the questionnaire.]*
> *You mentioned earlier that you had used drug(s) in the last 12 months. During this same period have you injected or had someone else inject you with a drug not prescribed by a doctor?*

The level of injecting use estimated by the BCS is likely to be on the conservative side. As the BCS samples households it excludes certain sections of the population: the homeless, prisoners, some of those with less traditional lifestyles and those in residential treatment for drug addiction. These tend to be the people thought to have higher levels of injecting.

Also, BCS prevalence estimates are subject to sampling errors, as only a sample of the total population is used. With rare behaviours, such as injecting, sampling errors can be large relative to the survey estimate.

Out of 10,940 people aged 16 – 59 who completed the drugs self-completion section, the BCS identified 22 injectors (0.1%). This represents three per cent of those who used a drug in the last year.

The 22 injectors identified were predominantly white (20), male (15), older (mean age = 34), single (10) and of low socio-economic status (10 users estimated their total household income as less than £5,000). In contrast with the stereotype of injecting drug users, about half (10) were in employment. As these injectors were sampled through households, they are likely to be more stable users of prohibited drugs, leading less problematic lifestyles than are usually associated with injecting. The injectors were also concentrated in Aspiring and Striving ACORN areas (4 and 12 respectively).

No clear patterns of drug use emerged. It is important to remember that the wording of the injecting question did not allow respondents to indicate which drugs they had actually injected. Drugs were used in the last year with the following frequencies: cannabis (14), amphetamines (12), ecstasy

(9), steroids (8), magic mushrooms (8), heroin (7), cocaine (7), unknown pill (7), tranquillisers (6), crack (6), methadone (6), poppers (5), LSD (4), smoke unknown (4), glue (4) and Semeron (2).

Although numbers are very small, and therefore firm conclusions cannot be drawn, the current data indicates that injectors had a low level of alcohol consumption (16 injectors never or infrequently drank), unlike most other drug users (Ramsay and Percy, 1996).

Some regional variations were also noted; five injectors were from London, five from the North West and six from Yorkshire and Humberside. The remainder were in the East Midlands (2), the South West (2), West Midlands (1) and Wales (1). These results appear broadly in line with other surveys. Leitner et al. (1993) found that "*no more than three per cent of respondents injected an unprescribed drug in London (Lewisham) and Nottingham*". Glasgow and Bradford, the other two cities involved, had lower rates of injecting in their main samples (1% and 2% respectively). Strang et al., (1992) found that in recent years smoking heroin had replaced injecting as the main form of drug use, with many moving to injecting at a later stage. Therefore, it is unsurprising that our sample of injectors are predominantly older users.

References

Aldridge, J., Parker, H. and Measham, F. (1995). *Drugs Pathways in the 1990s: adolescents' decision-making about illicit drug use.* Unpublished report to Central Drugs Prevention Unit, Home Office.

Balding, J. (1995). *Young People in 1994.* University of Exeter: Schools Health Education Unit.

Barclay, G., Drew, C., Hatton, R. and Abbot, C., eds. (1993). *Information on the Criminal Justice System in England and Wales.* London: Home Office.

CACI (1993). *ACORN User Guide.* London: CACI.

Elliott, D., Huizinga, D. and Menard, S. (1989). *Multiple Problem Youth: delinquency, substance health and mental health problems.* New York: Springer-Verlag.

Farrington, D. (1986). 'Age and crime', in M Tonry and N Morris (eds), *Crime and Justice. Annual Review of Research,* vol 7, pp. 189-250. Chicago: University of Chicago Press.

Farrington, D.(1995). 'The development of offending and antisocial behaviour from childhood: key findings from the Cambridge Study in Delinquent Development', *Journal of Child Psychology and Psychiatry* 36, pp.929 – 964.

FitzGerald, M. and Hales, C. (1996). *Ethnic Minorities, Victimisation and Racial Harassment: findings from the 1988 and 1992 British Crime Surveys.* Home Office Research Study 154. London: Home Office.

Grace, S. (1996). *Public Attitudes to Drug-Related Crime.* Research Findings 41. London: Home Office.

Graham, J. and Bowling, B. (1995). *Young People and Crime.* Home Office Research Study 145. London: Home Office.

Hales, J. and Stratford, N. (1997). *1996 British Crime Survey Technical Report.* London: SCPR.

Harrison, L. (1995). 'Trends and patterns of illicit drug use in the USA: implications for policy'. *International Journal of Drug Policy* 6, pp. 113-127.

HEA/BMRB International. (1997). *Drug Use in England: results of the 1995 National Drugs Campaign Survey.* London: Health Education Authority.

HEA/BMRB International. (1996). *Drug Realities: National Drugs Campaign Survey [1995], summary of key findings.* London: Health Education Authority.

Her Majesty's Government. (1995). *Tackling Drugs Together: a strategy for England 1995-1998.* London: HMSO.

Home Office. (1996). *Statistics of Drug Addicts Notified to the Home Office, United Kingdom, 1995.* London: Home Office.

Home Office. (1997). *Persistent Drug-Misusing Offenders.* Research Findings 50. London: Home Office.

ISDD. (1997). *Drug Misuse in Britain 1996.* London: ISDD.

Kandel, D. and Logan, J. (1984). 'Patterns of drug use from adolescence to young adulthood: 1. Periods of risk for initiation, continued use and discontinuation'. *American Journal of Public Health* 74, pp. 660-666.

Leitner, M., Shapland, J. and Wiles, P. (1993). *Drug Usage and Drugs Prevention.* London: HMSO.

Measham, F. (1996). 'The "big bang" approach to sessional drinking: changing patterns to sessional drinking amongst young people in North West England'. *Addiction Research* 4, pp. 283-299.

Miller, P. and Plant, M. (1996). 'Drinking, smoking and illicit drug use among 15 and 16 year olds in the United Kingdom'. *British Medical Journal* 313, pp. 394-397.

Mirrlees-Black, C., Mayhew, P. and Percy, A. (1996). *The 1996 British Crime Survey England and Wales.* Home Office Statistical Bulletin 19/96. London: Home Office.

Moore, D. and Polsgrove, L. (1991). 'Disabilities, developmental handicaps and substance use: a review'. *International Journal of the Addictions* 26, pp. 65-90.

Mott, J. and Mirrlees-Black, C. (1995). *Self-Reported Drug Misuse in England and Wales: findings from the 1992 British Crime Survey.* Research and Planning Unit Paper 89. London: Home Office.

Parker, H. and Bottomley, T. (1996). *Crack Cocaine and Drugs-Crime Careers.* Occasional Paper Series. London: Home Office.

Parker, H. and Kirby, P. (1996). *Methadone Maintenance and Crime Reduction on Merseyside.* Crime Detection and Prevention Series Paper 72. London: Home Office.

Parker, H. and Measham, F. (1994). 'Pick'n'mix: changing patterns of illicit drug use amongst 1990s adolescents', *Drugs: Education, Prevention and Policy* 1, pp. 5-13.

Parker, H., Measham, F. and Aldridge, F. (1995). *Drugs Futures: changing patterns of drug use amongst English youth.* London: ISDD.

Parker, H. and Newcombe, R. (1987). 'Heroin and acquisitive crime in an English community'. *British Journal of Sociology* 38, pp. 331-350.

Power, R. (1995). *Coping with Illicit Drug Use.* London: Tufnell Press.

Power, R., Power, T. and Gibson, N. (1996). 'Attitudes and experience of drug use amongst a group of London teenagers'. *Drugs: Education, Prevention and Policy* 3, pp. 71-80.

Ramsay, M. (1994a). 'Drug use and acquisitive crime: troubling riddles'. *Drugs Prevention News,* July 1994, p. 3.

Ramsay, M. (1994b). 'Legalising illicit drugs: what the public thinks'. *Focus on Police Research and Development,* No. 5, pp. 5-7.

Ramsay, M. and Percy, A. (1996). *Drug Misuse Declared: results of the 1994 British Crime Survey.* Home Office Research Study 151. London: Home Office.

Ramsay, M. and Percy, A. (1997) '*A national household survey of drug misuse in Britain: a decade of development'.* Addiction, 92, pp. 931–937

Rutter, M. and Smith, D. (1995). 'Towards causal explanations of time trends in psychosocial disorders of young people'. *In M Rutter and D Smith (eds), Psychosocial Disorders in Young People: time trends and their causes,* pp. 782-808. Chichester: John Wiley.

Shiner, M. and Newburn, T. (1996). *Young People, Drugs and Peer Education: an evaluation of the Youth Awareness Programme (YAP).* Home Office Drugs Prevention Initiative, Paper 13. London: Home Office.

Smith, M. and Browne, F. (1992). *General Household Survey 1990.* London: HMSO.

Strang, J., Griffiths, P., Powis, B. and Gossop, M. (1992). 'First use of heroin: changes in route of administration over time', *British Medical Journal,* 9 May 1992, pp. 1222-1223.

Thomas, H. (1996). 'A community survey of adverse effects of cannabis use'. *Drug and Alcohol Dependence,* 42, pp. 201-207.

Wright, J. and Pearl, L. (1995). 'Knowledge and experience of young people regarding drug misuse, 1969-94'. *British Medical Journal,* 309, 7 January 1995, pp. 20-24.

Publications

List of research publications

A list of research reports for the last three years is provided below. A **full** list of publications is available on request from the Research and Statistics Directorate Information and Publications Group.

Home Office Research Studies (HORS)

133. **Intensive Probation in England and Wales: an evaluation.** George Mair, Charles Lloyd, Claire Nee and Rae Sibbett. 1994. xiv + 143pp. (0 11 341114 6).

134. **Contacts between Police and Public: findings from the 1992 British Crime Survey.** Wesley G Skogan. 1995. ix + 93pp. (0 11 341115 4).

135. **Policing low-level disorder: Police use of Section 5 of the Public Order Act 1986.** David Brown and Tom Ellis. 1994. ix + 69pp. (0 11 341116 2).

136. **Explaining reconviction rates: A critical analysis.** Charles Lloyd, George Mair and Mike Hough. 1995. xiv + 103pp. (0 11 341117 0).

137. **Case Screening by the Crown Prosecution Service: How and why cases are terminated.** Debbie Crisp and David Moxon. 1995. viii + 66pp. (0 11 341137 5).

138. **Public Interest Case Assessment Schemes.** Debbie Crisp, Claire Whittaker and Jessica Harris. 1995. x + 58pp. (0 11 341139 1).

139. **Policing domestic violence in the 1990s.** Sharon Grace. 1995. x + 74pp. (0 11 341140 5).

140. **Young people, victimisation and the police: British Crime Survey findings on experiences and attitudes of 12 to 15 year olds.** Natalie Aye Maung. 1995. xii + 140pp. (0 11 341150 2).

141. **The Settlement of refugees in Britain.** Jenny Carey-Wood, Karen Duke, Valerie Karn and Tony Marshall. 1995. xii + 133pp. (0 11 341145 6).

142. **Vietnamese Refugees since 1982.** Karen Duke and Tony Marshall. 1995. x + 62pp. (0 11 341147 2).

143. **The Parish Special Constables Scheme.** Peter Southgate, Tom Bucke and Carole Byron. 1995. x + 59pp. (1 85893 458 3).

144. **Measuring the Satisfaction of the Courts with the Probation Service.** Chris May. 1995. x + 76pp. (1 85893 483 4).

145. **Young people and crime.** John Graham and Benjamin Bowling. 1995. xv + 142pp. (1 85893 551 2).

146. **Crime against retail and manufacturing premises: findings from the 1994 Commercial Victimisation Survey.** Catriona Mirrlees-Black and Alec Ross. 1995. xi + 110pp. (1 85893 554 7).

147. **Anxiety about crime: findings from the 1994 British Crime Survey.** Michael Hough. 1995. viii + 92pp. (1 85893 553 9).

148. **The ILPS Methadone Prescribing Project.** Rae Sibbitt. 1996. viii + 69pp. (1 85893 485 0).

149. **To scare straight or educate? The British experience of day visits to prison for young people.** Charles Lloyd. 1996. xi + 60pp. (1 85893 570 9).

150. **Predicting reoffending for Discretionary Conditional Release.** John B Copas, Peter Marshall and Roger Tarling. 1996. vii + 49pp. (1 85893 576 8).

151. **Drug misuse declared: results of the 1994 British Crime Survey.** Malcom Ramsay and Andrew Percy. 1996. xv + 131pp. (1 85893 628 4).

152. **An Evaluation of the Introduction and Operation of the Youth Court.** David O'Mahony and Kevin Haines. 1996. viii + 70pp. (1 85893 579 2).

153. **Fitting supervision to offenders: assessment and allocation decisions in the Probation Service.** Ros Burnett. 1996. xi + 99pp. (1 85893 599 7).

155. **PACE: a review of the literature. The first ten years.** David Brown. 1997. xx + 281pp. (1 85893 603 9).

156. **Automatic Conditional Release: the first two years.** Mike Maguire, Brigitte Perroud and Peter Raynor. 1996. x + 114pp. (1 85893 659 4).

157. **Testing obscenity: an international comparison of laws and controls relating to obscene material.** Sharon Grace. 1996. ix + 46pp. (1 85893 672 1).

158. **Enforcing community sentences: supervisors' perspectives on ensuring compliance and dealing with breach.** Tom Ellis, Carol Hedderman and Ed Mortimer. 1996. x + 81pp. (1 85893 691 8).

160. **Implementing crime prevention schemes in a multi-agency setting: aspects of process in the Safer Cities programme.** Mike Sutton. 1996. x + 53pp. (1 85893 691 8).

161. **Reducing criminality among young people: a sample of relevant programmes in the United Kingdom.** David Utting. 1997. vi + 122pp. (1 85893 744 2).

162. **Imprisoned women and mothers.** Dianne Caddle and Debbie Crisp. 1996. xiii + 74pp. (1 85893 760 4).

163. **Curfew orders with electronic monitoring: an evaluation of the first twelve months of the trials in Greater Manchester, Norfolk and Berkshire, 1995 - 1996.** George Mair and Ed Mortimer. 1996. x + 50pp. (1 85893 765 5).

165. **Enforcing financial penalties.** Claire Whittaker and Alan Mackie. 1997. xii + 58pp. (1 85893 786 8).

166. **Assessing offenders' needs: assessment scales for the probation service.** Rosumund Aubrey and Michael Hough. x + 55pp.(1 85893 799 X).

167. **Offenders on probation.** George Mair and Chris May. 1997. xiv + 95pp. (1 85893 890 2).

168. **Managing courts effectively: The reasons for adjournments in magistrates' courts.** Claire Whittaker, Alan Mackie, Ruth Lewis and Nicola Ponikiewski. 1997. x + 37pp. (1 85893 804 X).

169. **Addressing the literacy needs of offenders under probation supervision.** Gwynn Davis et al. 1997. xiv + 109pp. (1 85893 889 9).

170. **Understanding the sentencing of women.** Carol Hedderman and Loraine Gelsthorpe. 1997. ix + 85pp. (1 85893 893 7).

171. **Changing offenders' attitudes and behaviour: what works?** Julie Vennard *et al*. 1997. x + 69pp. (1 85893 904 6).

Nos 159 and 164 not published yet.

Research and Planning Unit Papers (RPUP)

81. **The welfare needs of unconvicted prisoners.** Diane Caddle and Sheila White. 1994.

82. **Racially motivated crime: a British Crime Survey analysis.** Natalie Aye Maung and Catriona Mirrlees-Black. 1994.

83. **Mathematical models for forecasting Passport demand.** Andy Jones and John MacLeod. 1994.

84. **The theft of firearms.** John Corkery. 1994.

85. **Equal opportunities and the Fire Service.** Tom Bucke. 1994.

86. **Drug Education Amongst Teenagers: a 1992 British Crime Survey Analysis.** Lizanne Dowds and Judith Redfern. 1995.

87. **Group 4 Prisoner Escort Service: a survey of customer satisfaction.** Claire Nee. 1994.

88. **Special Considerations: Issues for the Management and Organisation of the Volunteer Police.** Catriona Mirrlees-Black and Carole Byron. 1995.

89. **Self-reported drug misuse in England and Wales: findings from the 1992 British Crime Survey.** Joy Mott and Catriona Mirrlees-Black. 1995.

90. **Improving bail decisions: the bail process project, phase 1.** John Burrows, Paul Henderson and Patricia Morgan. 1995.

91. **Practitioners' views of the Criminal Justice Act: a survey of criminal justice agencies.** George Mair and Chris May. 1995.

92. **Obscene, threatening and other troublesome telephone calls to women in England and Wales: 1982-1992.** Wendy Buck, Michael Chatterton and Ken Pease. 1995.

93. **A survey of the prisoner escort and custody service provided by Group 4 and by Securicor Custodial Services.** Diane Caddle. 1995.

Research Findings

8. **Findings from the International Crime Survey.** Pat Mayhew. 1994.

9. **Fear of Crime: Findings from the 1992 British Crime Survey.** Catriona Mirrlees-Black and Natalie Aye Maung. 1994.

10. **Does the Criminal Justice system treat men and women differently?** Carol Hedderman and Mike Hough. 1994.

11. **Participation in Neighbourhood Watch: Findings from the 1992 British Crime Survey.** Lizanne Dowds and Pat Mayhew. 1994.

12. **Explaining Reconviction Rates: A Critical Analysis.** Charles Lloyd, George Mair and Mike Hough. 1995.

13. **Equal opportunities and the Fire Service.** Tom Bucke. 1994.

14. **Trends in Crime: Findings from the 1994 British Crime Survey.** Pat Mayhew, Catriona Mirrlees-Black and Natalie Aye Maung. 1994.

15. **Intensive Probation in England and Wales: an evaluation**. George Mair, Charles Lloyd, Claire Nee and Rae Sibbitt. 1995.

16. **The settlement of refugees in Britain**. Jenny Carey-Wood, Karen Duke, Valerie Karn and Tony Marshall. 1995.

17. **Young people, victimisation and the police: British Crime Survey findings on experiences and attitudes of 12- to 15-year-olds.** Natalie Aye Maung. 1995.

18. **Vietnamese Refugees since 1982.** Karen Duke and Tony Marshall. 1995.

19. **Supervision of Restricted Patients in the Community.** Suzanne Dell and Adrian Grounds. 1995.

20. **Videotaping children's evidence: an evaluation.** Graham Davies, Clare Wilson, Rebecca Mitchell and John Milsom. 1995.

21. **The mentally disordered and the police.** Graham Robertson, Richard Pearson and Robert Gibb. 1995.

22. **Preparing records of taped interviews.** Andrew Hooke and Jim Knox. 1995.

23. **Obscene, threatening and other troublesome telephone calls to women: Findings from the British Crime Survey.** Wendy Buck, Michael Chatterton and Ken Pease. 1995.

24. **Young people and crime.** John Graham and Ben Bowling. 1995.

25. **Anxiety about crime: Findings from the 1994 British Crime Survey.** Michael Hough. 1995.

26. **Crime against retail premises in 1993.** Catriona Mirrlees-Black and Alec Ross. 1995.

27. **Crime against manufacturing premises in 1993.** Catriona Mirrlees-Black and Alec Ross. 1995.

28. **Policing and the public: findings from the 1994 British Crime Survey.** Tom Bucke. 1995.

29. **The Child Witness Pack – An Evaluation.** Joyce Plotnikoff and Richard Woolfson. 1995.

30. **To scare straight or educate? The British experience of day visits to prison for young people.** Charles Lloyd. 1996.

31. **The ADT drug treatment programme at HMP Downview – a preliminary evaluation.** Elaine Player and Carol Martin. 1996.

32. **Wolds remand prison – an evaluation.** Keith Bottomley, Adrian James, Emma Clare and Alison Liebling. 1996.

33. **Drug misuse declared: results of the 1994 British Crime Survey.** Malcolm Ramsay and Andrew Percy. 1996.

34. **Crack cocaine and drugs-crime careers.** Howard Parker and Tim Bottomley. 1996.

35.   **Imprisonment for fine default.** David Moxon and Claire Whittaker. 1996.

36.   **Fine impositions and enforcement following the Criminal Justice Act 1993.** Elizabeth Charman, Bryan Gibson, Terry Honess and Rod Morgan. 1996.

37.   **Victimisation in prisons.** Ian O'Donnell and Kimmett Edgar. 1996.

38   **Mothers in prison.** Dianne Caddle and Debbie Crisp. 1997.

39.   **Ethnic minorities, victimisation and racial harassment.** Marian Fitzgerald and Chris Hale. 1996.

40.   **Evaluating joint performance management between the police and the Crown Prosecution Service.** Andrew Hooke, Jim Knox and David Portas. 1996.

41.   **Public attitudes to drug-related crime.** Sharon Grace. 1996.

42.   **Domestic burglary schemes in the safer cities programme.** Paul Ekblom, Ho Law and Mike Sutton. 1996.

43.   **Pakistani women's experience of domestic violence in Great Britain.** Salma Choudry. 1996.

44.   **Witnesses with learning disabilities.** Andrew Sanders, Jane Creaton, Sophia Bird and Leanne Weber. 1997.

45.   **Does treating sex offenders reduce reoffending?** Carol Hedderman and Darren Sugg. 1996.

46.   **Re-education programmes for violent men - an evaluation.** Russell Dobash, Rebecca Emerson Dobash, Kate Cavanagh and Ruth Lewis. 1996.

47.   **Sentencing without a pre-sentence report.** Nigel Charles, Claire Whittaker and Caroline Ball. 1997.

48   **Magistrates' views of the probation service.** Chris May. 1997.

49.   **PACE ten years on: a review of the research.** David Brown. 1997.

50.   **Persistent drug-misusing offenders.** Malcolm Ramsay. 1997.

51. **Curfew orders with electronic monitoring: the first twelve months.** 1997. Ed Mortimer and George Mair.

52. **Police cautioning in the 1990s.** 1997. Roger Evans and Rachel Evans.

53. **A reconviction study of HMP Grendon Therapeutic Community.** Peter Marshall. 1997.

55. **The prevalence of convictions for sexual offending.** Peter Marshall. 1997.

57. **The 1996 International Crime Victimisation Survey.** 1997. Pat Mayhew and Philip White.

Nos 54, 55 and 56 not yet published.

Research Bulletin (no longer produced)

The Research Bulletin contains short articles on recent research. Back issues are available on request.

Occasional Papers

Measurement of caseload weightings associated with the Children Act. Richard J. Gadsden and Graham J. Worsdale. 1994. (Available from the RSD Information and Publications Group.)

Managing difficult prisoners: The Lincoln and Hull special units. Professor Keith Bottomley, Professor Norman Jepson, Mr Kenneth Elliott and Dr Jeremy Coid. 1994. (Available from the RSD Information and Publications Group.)

The Nacro diversion initiative for mentally disturbed offenders: an account and an evaluation. Home Office, NACRO and Mental Health Foundation. 1994. (Available from the RSD Information and Publications Group.)

Probation Motor Projects in England and Wales. J P Martin and Douglas Martin. 1994.

Community-based treatment of sex offenders: an evaluation of seven treatment programmes. R Beckett, A Beech, D Fisher and A S Fordham. 1994.

Videotaping children's evidence: an evaluation. Graham Davies, Clare Wilson, Rebecca Mitchell and John Milsom. 1995.

Managing the needs of female prisoners. Allison Morris, Chris Wilkinson, Andrea Tisi, Jane Woodrow and Ann Rockley. 1995.

Local information points for volunteers. Michael Locke, Nick Richards, Lorraine Down, Jon Griffiths and Roger Worgan. 1995.

Mental disorder in remand prisoners. Anthony Maden, Caecilia J. A. Taylor, Deborah Brooke and John Gunn. 1996.

An evaluation of prison work and training. Frances Simon and Claire Corbett. 1996.

The Impact of the National Lottery on the Horse-Race Betting Levy. Simon Field. 1996.

The impact of the National Lottery on the Horserace betting levy: Second report. Simon Field and James Dunmore. 1997.

Requests for Publications

Home Office Research Studies from 143 onwards, *Research and Planning Unit Papers, Research Findings and Research Bulletins* can be requested, **subject to availability**, from:

Research and Statistics Directorate
Information and Publications Group
Room 201, Home Office
50 Queen Anne's Gate
London SW1H 9AT
Telephone: 0171-273 2084
Fascimile: 0171-222 0211
Internet: http://www.open.gov.uk/home_off/rsdhome.htm
E-mail: rsd.ho apollo@gtnet.gov.uk

Occasional Papers can be purchased from:
Home Office
Publications Unit
50 Queen Anne's Gate
London SW1H 9AT
Telephone: 0171 273 3072

Home Office Research Studies prior to 143 can be purchased from:

HMSO Publications Centre

(Mail, fax and telephone orders only)
PO Box 276, London SW8 5DT
Telephone orders: 0171-873 9090
General enquiries: 0171-873 0011
(queuing system in operation for both numbers)
Fax orders: 0171-873 8200

*And also from **HMSO Bookshops***